D0387808

The Loyalty Link

The Loyalty Link

How Loyal Employees
Create Loyal Customers

Dennis G. McCarthy

JOHN WILEY & SONS, INC.

New York • Chichester • Weinheim • Brisbane • Singapore • Toronto

Library of Congress Cataloging-in-Publication Data:

McCarthy, Dennis G.
   The loyalty link : how loyal employees create loyal customers /
Dennis G. McCarthy.
     p.   cm.
   Includes index.
   ISBN 0-471-16389-9 (cloth : alk. paper)
   1. Customer relations.   2. Employee loyalty.   I. Title.
HF5415.5.M183   1997
658.8′12—dc21   96-46702

Printed in the United States of America

10 9 8 7 6 5 4 3 2 1

For Sarah, Michael, and Allison

Acknowledgments

───────────── ⚜ ⚜ ⚜ ⚜ ─────────────

When I started lecturing on the topic of loyalty, I was amazed at the reaction I received. Audiences around the country would nod in approval at the topic, but then say that "it couldn't be done"—not when you consider how cynical and mistrustful today's workforce has become. This book is my answer to the skeptics.

This book wouldn't exist today if not for the kindness and support of many people. My first debt of gratitude is to those who graciously consented to be interviewed and who shared their ideas and thoughts with me. Since they are mentioned throughout the book I will introduce them at that time.

My second debt of gratitude goes to my colleagues at Paradigm Group who supported the intensive effort required to turn this book into reality. My thanks especially go to Gary Jackson and Charlie Lambert for their willingness to pick up the slack I occasionally created in this process. I am also grateful to our incredible staff, Dena Vauiso, Carol Morabito, Laura Morabito, and Stephanie Garcia for their willingness to take care of the myriad details that are part of book writing, as well as David Harrison for his thorough research.

I am also indebted to my friend and confidant Barry Tarshis who helped shepherd the writing process smoothly and clearly, helping to translate my ideas and thoughts into readable language and useful ideas.

And finally I want to thank my wife, Sarah and my children, Allison and Michael, for their patience and love during the times that I was not available while working on this book. Without their love and encouragement there would be no *Loyalty Link*.

Contents

Introduction

꿏 꿏 꿏 꿏

few years ago, according to a story often told at
customer service training seminars, a family whose
house had just been devastated by a fire was
standing on the front lawn, looking grimly at the charred
remnants of their home when a pizza delivery truck pulled
into their driveway. "There must be some mistake," one of
the family members said as the driver walked up to them
carrying two large pizza boxes. "We didn't order any pizzas.
We don't even have a phone anymore."

"It's no mistake," the young man said. He explained that
he had driven by earlier and seen what had happened. "So
my boss and I thought that, by now, you probably needed
something to eat. Please accept it with our compliments.
And if it's not the kind of pizza you like, I'd be happy to go
back and get you a different kind."

Whether this story actually happened I can't vouch for.
As with most stories of this nature, it's undoubtedly a com-
posite of a number of stories, whose particulars keep
changing with each retelling.

Still, this story invariably strikes a responsive chord with
businesspeople who are struggling more than ever before
to sharpen the competitive edge of their companies by im-
proving the quality of the service their employees provide
to customers. If nothing else, the story exemplifies a level
of customer service that clearly goes beyond the norm, that
originates, not from the pages of a policy handbook, but

from the heart of a caring person; it's the kind of service that you can't really train or even pay people to deliver. The story brings to light the sort of attitude and commitment that most companies would dearly like to instill in their employees—qualities that produce actions that do more than satisfy customers and result in something far more critical to a company's success: customer loyalty.

Don't misunderstand; I'm not suggesting that the only reason the hero of this story (and his employer) decided to come to the aid of a family whose house had burned down is that they figured it would be good for business. The fact remains, though, that the benefits of this thoughtful gesture—and indeed any thoughtful gestures directed toward current or would-be customers—cut both ways. On the one hand, the simple act of cooking and delivering a pizza helped a family in need. On the other hand, it created a bond between the pizza parlor and the unfortunate family that isn't likely to dissolve in the near future. Think about it: Who do you think this family is likely to call, once it gets back on its feet, when somebody wants to order a pizza?

The Anatomy of a Good Deed

I have told this story innumerable times in many of the seminars I conduct, and I've always been fascinated by the response it tends to elicit. The most common comment, by far, is, "How do I get in touch with that delivery guy—I'll hire him on the spot." The implication being, of course, that it is next to impossible these days to find employees, particularly at the entry level, who bring to their jobs the sense of caring and commitment personified by the hero of the pizza story.

Nevertheless, it is an understandable response. It's no secret that most companies today, especially those in the service industry, are finding it harder and harder to attract and keep employees who can meet the standards of customer service that we all know are necessary today to stay competitive in most businesses. And there is no shortage of theories, either, as to why this state of affairs exists.

But logical as this response may be in light of today's business environment, it is not, I submit, the most productive one. A much more productive response to this situation would be to ask the following question: What were the conditions, generally speaking, that fostered the events described in this story? True, the young man deserves our admiration, but let's give at least some of the credit to the delivery man's employer.

I'll explain what I mean. Let's assume the basic events of this story are true, and that the person who owned or managed the pizza parlor was not a character straight out of Dickens. This means that when the young delivery man returned to the pizza parlor and began talking about the unfortunate family, the owner didn't shrug his shoulders and growl something like, "So what? What are we, the Red Cross?"

We can also assume, based on the general outline of this story, that the owner didn't insist that his delivery man pay for the pizza that was earmarked for the family in need and didn't tell him that the delivery would have to be done on the employee's time.

Going a step further—again, all of this is hypothetical— assume that one of the main reasons the young pizza delivery man was hired in the first place is that the owner recognized in this young man the qualities that compelled him to take the actions he took. Which leads to the next assumption, that the owner of this pizza parlor took the time to think about the sort of person he needed, then took specific steps to hire somebody of quality instead of going the "Just get me a warm body" route. Assume, too, that the pizza parlor itself was a pleasant place to work: that the working conditions were healthy and safe, that there was a sense of caring between the owners and the employees, and that the employees were being paid a reasonable salary.

In other words, the good deed that is the subject of the story was not a random event. It didn't simply "happen." It occurred because of an environment that did more than simply *allow* it to happen; it actually *fostered* it—made it more likely to happen. This kind of environment is characterized by the phrase I have chosen as the title of this book—*The Loyalty Link*.

The Loyalty Link Defined

The loyalty link is the connection I am going to draw between a company and its customers and between a company and its employees. It becomes apparent that such a link exists as soon as you begin to compare survey numbers relating to two different categories of satisfaction: customer satisfaction and employee satisfaction.

The correlations are striking. Whenever you find a company whose customers report an exceptionally high level of satisfaction, almost invariably that company also has high levels of employee satisfaction. And along with that high level of employee satisfaction come other benefits, such as high productivity, low turnover, and high operating efficiency. By the same token, whenever you come across a company or business in which customer satisfaction measures well below the average, you generally find correspondingly low levels of employee satisfaction, with all its concomitant and expensive baggage—high turnover, poor levels of quality, and the like.

The purpose of this book is to take a close look at this link between customer loyalty and employee loyalty, and by doing so, show you how you can create a loyalty link in your own company or business. The book has a pragmatic focus. I do not intend to simply lecture you about how important it is these days that everybody in your organization be committed to the highest possible standards of customer service. Nor is this book designed to spell out specifically for you all the various things your employees need to do in order to deliver the level of customer service that is required today if you hope to keep your customers from being wooed away by your competitors.

The focus of this book is on you and what you are doing (or ought to be doing) as the owner or key manager of a business to put the loyalty link to work for you.

The book is based on three key premises:

■ To prevail in today's marketplace, you have to do more than simply "satisfy" your customers. You have to *exceed* their expectations, satisfying them in a way that captures—and *maintains*—their loyalty. You need to create a bond strong enough to withstand the efforts of your competitors to woo your customers away from you.

■ The only way you can bridge the gap between customer service that simply satisfies and service that exceeds expectations (and therefore builds customer loyalty) is to have employees who are willing and able to provide the extra measure of dedication, care, and effort that represents the difference between customer service per se and exceptional levels of customer service. I call this extra measure "discretionary effort": It's what employees *choose* to do as opposed to what their job descriptions *obligate* them to do.

■ If you want your employees to put forth the discretionary effort that ensures loyalty, you need to focus as much on your employees as you do on your customers. And in the same way that you can no longer afford to take customers for granted in today's competitive marketplace, neither can you afford to take your employees for granted. Simply put, any customer service initiative that doesn't take into account your employees—who they are, how they're trained, how they're treated, how aware they are of your customers' needs, and how easy (or difficult) the culture and the working environment in your company makes it for them to meet those needs— is doomed from the start.

A Real-World Strategy

Let me point out at this early juncture that I am under no illusions. As a business consultant, I am intimately aware of what has been going on in companies throughout America over the last 20 years, and I am familiar with the bind that many companies find themselves in today. The irony couldn't be plainer. At the same time creating customer loyalty has become the number one challenge for many companies today, maintaining employee loyalty has never been more difficult.

The loyalty crisis you hear so much about today isn't a fabrication. Climate studies done in organizations across the country point to an across-the-board decline in the loyalty employees feel toward their jobs and employers. The decline has been charted since the mid-1960s, paralleling the general decline in the confidence that Americans feel toward most institutions. But the level of dissatisfaction that employees feel toward their jobs and their employees has accelerated dramatically over the past 10 years, for reasons we're all familiar with. The downsizings that peaked in the early 1990s have pretty much wiped out the old-fashioned notion of "job security," even in companies in which job security has always been a given. But an equally important factor is the intense pressure the "survivors" of these downsizings are now feeling as the result of having a larger job load to handle each day—with less support to do so.

I have more to say in a later chapter about downsizing and the impact it has had not only on employee loyalty but on customer loyalty as well. For now, suffice it to say that the overall picture, bleak as it may seem on the surface, may not be as hopeless as some people have painted it. The sky isn't falling—not just yet. Yes, it is getting tougher and tougher to attract and keep good customers, and it's getting tougher and tougher to attract and keep the kind of employees you need to generate and maintain customer loyalty. But some companies are meeting both challenges. You will be reading about many of these companies throughout this book, and it will probably surprise you to discover that you could be implementing in your own company many of the things they're doing, without spending as much money or putting forth as much effort as you may think necessary.

But I don't want to make promises I can't keep. What I have to offer in this book isn't "cookie-cutter" advice. And I am not going to pretend—particularly at this early stage of the book—that creating a customer-focused loyalty link in your company is easy. Chances are, many of the ideas in this book will fly in the face of attitudes that are deeply entrenched in both you and in your company culture. You may have a very difficult time, for example, seeing the bottom-line value of doing all the little extra things that can mean the difference between a satisfied customer and a loyal customer. You may question the wisdom of giving your employees the freedom, the flexibility, and the autonomy that is required if indeed you want them to put forth that extra discretionary effort that underlies exceptional customer service. And you may not be willing to invest the time and the effort to make the fundamental changes necessary if your company is going to be customer-driven in the true sense of the word.

However, I will guarantee you this. If you're willing to try just a few of the approaches I describe in this book, and give them time to "take hold," you will see measurable differences in the way your employees go about their jobs and, more important, in the way they deal with your customers. And you will experience other benefits: Your employees will bring more enthusiasm and commitment to their jobs. Turnover will decline. Customers will no longer be as tempted to switch to competitors. Profits will increase. And most important, perhaps, you and your employees will rediscover the fun and passion that got you started in business in the first place. And that alone may be worth the effort.

Chapter 1

꘏꘏ ꘏꘏ ꘏꘏ ꘏꘏

Customer Satisfaction

The Panacea That Isn't Working

oes this sound familiar? You're finishing a dinner at a restaurant you've never been to before when the manager or owner materializes at your table with a smile and the inevitable question: "How was everything?"

If you're like most people, you don't really say what's on your mind: that nothing was terribly *wrong* with your dinner—nothing you are compelled to complain about—but there wasn't anything worth getting excited about, either. You don't let the manager know, for instance, that while the salad was okay, it was just a trifle soggy; that the veal, while tasty, could have been, well, just a little more tender; and that the service, while friendly enough, could have been a lot smoother.

Instead, you are polite. You figure you're not going to come back again, so why make a big deal of things. You tell the owner or manager that everything was fine, just fine. The owner smiles, thanks you, and walks away, comfortable in the knowledge that the restaurant has done its job and gained a satisfied customer—somebody who will come back again. You, the "satisfied" customer, walk out the door with no intention of ever coming back. To make matters worse for the owner, when friends ask you for your opinion of the restaurant, you become what is known among customer service specialists as a "terrorist." You tell everyone who asks you how bad the restaurant was. In fact, you exaggerate the faults you didn't reveal when you responded to the owner's question that everything was all right. Consequently, you make it unlikely that your friends will ever become customers either. You can only hope for the sake of the future of this restaurant that it doesn't have too many customers who were as "satisfied" as you were, or the restaurant isn't long for this world.

The Way It Was

Until recently, it was generally taken for granted that if you polled your customers and found that most of them were "satisfied," you could pretty much relax. You could assume that you were doing the right things; and that when those customers were in the market for another car, insurance policy, or dress, or wanted to buy more stock, they would come to you. After all, why would customers who were satisfied be anything less than loyal?

By the same token, you could assume that as long as your customers were coming back to you time and again, they were loyal—that you could count on their repeat business, without having to go out of your way to retain their allegiance.

All of which helps to explain why the conventional wisdom during the 1970s and 1980s was that it didn't pay to focus too much of your time, resources, and energy on activities geared to *increase* the satisfaction of those customers who were already satisfied—already in your pocket, so to speak. What was the point of it? You already had their business locked up. Sure, you had to keep in touch with them—make sure you sent them a nice Christmas card every year and that sort of thing. But if you were really shrewd and strategic, you took the time, the money, and resources you might invest in increasing the satisfaction level of existing customers, and instead applied it to activities geared to one of two things: attracting *new* customers, or making dissatisfied customers happier.

So much for how things used to be and what people used to think. We now know that the conventional wisdom of the 1970s and 1980s no longer applies, not when customers are more sophisticated; not when they have more choices than ever in most businesses; and not when technological advances have made it possible for competitors of all sizes to zero in relentlessly on your customers, with one objective: to get them to leave you and join them. We know, for instance, that the link between customer satisfaction (as measured by how customers respond to surveys) and customer loyalty (as measured by actual customer behavior) is not nearly as direct as most people had once believed. And we know that what often appears on the surface as customer loyalty isn't loyalty at all in the true sense of the word: It can be more accurately described as customer tolerance; and we know that customers who manifest this particular type of loyalty are ripe candidates for defection.

As it happens, savvy CEOs have long questioned the practice of their senior managers to take satisfied customers for granted, but it wasn't until the early 1990s that there was any evidence that would warrant any change in thinking. The "smoking gun" in this instance can be traced to the analysis performed by the Xerox corporation on customer satisfaction data it had been gathering annually for many years from nearly 500,000 of its customers. Xerox, like most companies, had always organized its customer response surveys around a satisfaction scale of 1 to 5, and early in the process had set a corporate goal of 100 percent, or 4s. Xerox, in other words, was buying into the conventional view that as long as the company was producing moderately high levels of satisfaction, customers would remain loyal.

Not quite. In 1991, Xerox took a closer look at its numbers and made a surprising—and disquieting—discovery. They found that a high percentage of 4s—that is, customers who, by Xerox's own barometer, were "satisfied"—were not behaving the way they expected satisfied customers to behave. For one thing, they weren't grateful; when the time came to repurchase, they weren't coming back to Xerox. When the Xerox number crunchers looked closely, they found that loyalty rates among Xerox's 4s were only marginally higher than loyalty rates among customers whose satisfaction levels were in the high 3s and lower.

They found out something else, too, something even more important. They found an enormous loyalty gap between 4s and 5s. True, you would normally expect to find differences in the loyalty levels between customers who were simply "satisfied" (4s) and customers who were "completely satisfied" (5s). But what the Xerox analysis found was a gap far wider than anyone would have logically expected. Xerox's 5s weren't simply more loyal than 4s, they were *six* times more loyal. And, as Thomas O. Jones and W. Earl Sasser pointed out in the *Harvard Business Review* article "Why Satisfied Customers Defect" (Nov/Dec 1995), the implications of that gap were "profound." "Merely satisfying customers who have the freedom to make choices is not enough to make them loyal," Jones and Sasser observed in their own analysis of the Xerox study. "The only truly loyal customers are totally satisfied customers."

Variations on the Theme

The Xerox study was only the first of a series that have shed new light on what had previously been relatively unexplored territory: the link between customer satisfaction and customer loyalty. Studies in other companies and in other industries have since emerged that have reinforced the basic message of the original Xerox study—that the mountain you need to climb to build customer loyalty is a lot steeper and slicker than conventional wisdom had led everyone to believe. A series of studies carried out by the Boston-based consulting firm Bain & Company led Frederick F. Reichheld, one of Bain's directors, to report in the *Harvard Business Review* article "Loyalty-Based Management," (March–April, 1993) that, depending on the industry, the percentage of "satisfied" or "very satisfied" customers who nonetheless defect when the time comes to repurchase is between 65 percent and 85 percent. Reichheld pointed out, too, that in the automobile industry, less than half of those customers who say that they are satisfied with the car they bought stay loyal to the company from which they originally purchased the car.

So what's going on here? Why do satisfied customers defect? Is it simply, as many people argue, that we live in an age in which loyalty, as we have traditionally understood this value, is dead? Are we to believe that the only thing that really matters to most customers today is price, and that no matter what you do, if you can't match your competitors' prices, even your most loyal customers are going to jump ship?

No one could brand you a cynic for taking this position, for it can't be disputed that most customers today are far more price-conscious than ever before—and far more knowledgeable when it comes to determining where they're getting the most value. "It's an entirely different ball game today when it comes to dealing with customers," one of the floor salesmen at Ritar Ford, in Norwalk, Connecticut was saying recently. He explained that shoppers often come into the dealership loaded down with consumer research gathered from the Internet and other places, the net result being that many customers know almost to the nickel how much profit the dealership makes.

But it's not yet time to jump to conclusions—not now anyway. For it is one thing to say that conventional approaches to building customer loyalty don't work anymore in today's highly competitive environment, and something else again to state flatly that the only thing most customers are loyal to today is their wallets or pocketbooks. Price will always be a factor in consumer decisions, but it's by no means the only factor. The most successful automobile dealerships today, according to J.D. Powers surveys, are not attracting and keeping customers because they've priced their cars cheaper than everybody else. It's because they've developed powerful customer service programs that make the experience of owning and servicing the cars they sell measurably more pleasant than in other dealerships.

The principle holds true in other industries as well. Ritz-Carlton, the luxury hotel chain, didn't win the coveted Baldrige Award because its room rates are cheaper than the competition. As long as the economy remains reasonably healthy, there will always be a sizable segment of the American population—and it varies from one industry to the next—willing to pay a little extra (and the threshold, according to most studies, is between 10 and 15 percent), providing they're getting something of value in return.

But you wouldn't know this from observing the way many companies operate today. Faced with increasing competition and relentless pressure on profit margins, the knee-jerk reaction of many companies has been to shift the focus from the positive things they need to do to attract customers and to concentrate instead on cutting costs so that they can keep their prices as low as possible. What these companies are *not* doing is addressing the real reason they're losing business. And it's not solely because their customers are able to buy the same product or service someplace else, but because the companies themselves have lost sight of the most important factor in business— the totality of the customer experience: how the customers *feel* when they're buying the product, using the product, or looking for someone in your company who can help them solve a problem they have with the product.

Satisfaction and Loyalty: A Closer Look

Most of this book examines and explains what you need to do in your business—apart from lowering your prices—

to reach that critical point at which customer satisfaction begins to translate into customer loyalty. With this goal in mind, let's take a closer look at what we've learned about the satisfaction-loyalty connection, based on the data that have emerged from studies of the past five years.

The most important insight is one of semantics, specifically, how we define satisfaction. As used in customer satisfaction surveys, the term traditionally has been viewed as a positive attitude. It turns out, however, that many customers use the word satisfaction not so much to express the presence of a *positive* feeling but to communicate the absence of a *negative* feeling. Upon closer examination, the majority of "satisfied" customers in the typical customer satisfaction survey turn out to be neutral. They have no compelling reason to defect but no compelling reason either to remain with you. As Jones and Sasser put it, customers who fall into this category are "up for grabs."

Certainly, you can run a highly successful business today even if the majority of your customers fall into this neutral category. A lot depends on your competition—or, more specifically, on the choices that are open to your customers. If you operate the only gas station in Dry Gulch, a one-horse town in the middle of the Mojave Desert, you don't have to worry too much about any gap that might exist between those customers who are satisfied and those who are completely satisfied. When drivers need gas, they're going to come to you. And if your customers don't like the fact that the kid who pumps gas looks and acts like a character out of one of those slasher movies, or that your rest rooms haven't been cleaned since the Korean War, so what? Where else are these customers going to go?

A quick but relevant aside. One of the biggest problems private enterprise advocates are having today in Russia as well in other Eastern-bloc countries is instilling a genuine understanding of customer service in employees who formerly worked in companies run by the state but who now work for companies that must compete in the free market. This is not because these people are inherently less hospitable than, say, Americans. On the contrary, if you've ever been to Russia and been invited to someone's home, you know that this simply isn't true. The typical Russian family will knock themselves out to make a guest feel at home.

But going out of your way to be courteous and hospitable to people you deal with in commerce (as opposed to friends and family members) is an alien concept in a society in which consumers had no real options. Why would someone who wasn't being paid a decent salary anyway go out of his or her way to be cordial and helpful to a customer who had no place else to shop, no one to complain to, and who, if the roles were reversed, would be equally indifferent?

But let's get back to the here and now in America—in this case, to Dry Gulch and the gas station you own. Let us assume, for the sake of argument, that after having had a virtual lock on the gas business in your particular neck of the desert for all these years, you discover one day (as the companies in a number of recently deregulated industries have) that you have some competition. Suddenly, no more than two miles away, you have a competitor who is charging roughly the same price that you are for gas but is offering far more in the way of customer service extras— attendants who greet drivers warmly, a comfortable lounge where they can get the kids something cold to drink, and rest rooms that are clean and sparkling. Given this new set of circumstances, how long do you think it will be before you begin to see these differences where it counts the most—in your cash register?

And here, in short, is the problem with a customer base made up primarily of customers who are satisfied in the neutral sense of the word. These customers manifest what Thomas Jones and Earl Sasser describe as "false loyalty," based on expedience and limited choices, and not on deep-rooted attitudes. As such, these customers tend to exhibit the following characteristics:

■ They feel little or no brand or organization loyalty or attachment.

■ They have little or no tolerance for mistakes or problems.

■ They are open and vulnerable to any number of influences (price or policy changes or differences, minor competitive advantages in number of features, location, and the like).

Customers who are merely satisfied (that is, not *dissatisfied*), in short, are highly unpredictable. No force holds them where they are. And because their satisfaction isn't rooted in anything that can resist a strong pull, it doesn't take much to attract their attention and draw them away.

I could cite any number of specific instances that illustrate the folly that Sasser and Jones address in their article—the pitfall of equating customer satisfaction with customer loyalty—but the one example that comes immediately to mind is what happened to IBM in the personal computer market. You might recall that in the early to mid-1980s, when the personal computer business was still in its infancy, IBM all but owned the PC business market. Indeed the terms IBM and PC became almost synonymous, much as the brand name Kleenex has long been synonymous with tissues, or Levi's with jeans.

In retrospect, though, it is obvious that the reason IBM dominated this market early in the game was not that it was turning out superior products or even that it was doing an unusually good job of meeting the needs and expectations of its customers. It was more that IBM had a great deal of money to spend on marketing and sales, coupled with the fact that most computer buyers knew very little about the products they were buying. The typical business customer needed the reassurance that the IBM name provided. I can recall years ago, when I was working for a major corporation, that the people responsible for buying mainframes wouldn't give non-IBM salespeople the time of day. Their reasoning: "No one ever got fired for buying IBM." And that attitude permeated the IBM PC group as well. So it is that IBM's PC customers may have been satisfied all right, but the satisfaction wasn't deep enough to produce genuine loyalty.

We all know what happened. Within time, the clone companies—Compaq and Dell, to name two—began to edge their way into the marketplace. And because their products clearly outperformed the early IBM PCs, and did so at a lower price, many of the "loyal" IBM customers began to defect, slowly at first but eventually in droves. Yes, Big Blue did eventually rebound, but it has never come close to recapturing the dominance it once enjoyed in the PC market. They committed the cardinal sin of business: They took their customers for granted.

Customer Loyalty: The Bottom Line

If it is true, as most people now believe, that the link between customer satisfaction and customer loyalty is not as direct as was once commonly thought, it is reasonable to ask ourselves how much it really matters. You could well argue that the amount of time and effort it takes to raise customers from the "satisfied" category to the "completely satisfied" category doesn't make sense when you're looking at it in pure bottom-line terms. After all, it takes time to recruit, hire, and train employees who do more than simply go through the motions—and you usually have to pay them more, too. Further, it sometimes costs money to buy equipment that makes it easier for you to stay in touch with your customers. Why bother?

Why indeed? Let's start with the most basic of reasons: money. Money in your company's pocket. Studies by Bain & Company, among others, have shown consistently that it costs far more to attract new customers than it does to retain the customers you already have. Jerry Florence, vice president of communications for Nissan Motor Company, estimates that it costs his company anywhere from 6 to 10 times as much money to attract a new customer as it does to retain an existing customer; and Nissan, according to our own studies, represents the rule, not the exception.

If you are like most people, your survival depends in large part on your ability to acquire new customers, forgetting for the moment the loyalty of your existing customers. The issue here, though, is balance. If you're losing existing customers at the same rate you're attracting new customers, the extra money you have to spend on acquisition will ultimately catch up to you. That's why Florence, among others, believes that the bottom line in many companies is more sensitive to customer defections than it is to new customer acquisition.

But the economic implications of customer loyalty go well beyond the costs normally associated with acquiring new customers. An equally important—and often over-looked—aspect of this connection is how much more money it takes to service and support new customers com-pared to the money and resources it takes to service and support longtime customers.

One of the most cogent analyses of how this cost differ-ential affects your company's bottom line can be found in Frederick F. Reichheld's book *The Loyalty Effect* (Harvard Business School Press, 1996). Reichheld based his analysis on the view that many costs routinely incurred when you are selling your product or service to a new customer are frequently "hidden"; that is, you can't identify them through conventional accounting and bookkeeping practices.

Reichheld concedes that the disparity is more clearly ev-ident in some businesses and professions than in others, but he nonetheless offers a wealth of convincing evidence to reinforce his premise: that, in the final analysis, selling to your existing (and presumably loyal) customers is far more profitable than selling to your new customers, every-thing else being equal. In the financial planning business, for instance, it is not unusual for financial planners to spend five times as many hours on a first-time client than on an existing client; and most financial planners work on a fee or commission basis, not on an hourly basis. And even in companies where you wouldn't normally assume a big difference between the cost of servicing a recent customer and the cost of servicing an existing customer, disparities still find their way to the bottom line—and in surprising ways. After analyzing the costs and efficiency levels of a large industrial laundry company in Europe, Reichheld's firm found "large differences" on those routes comprised primarily of stable, long-term customers and those made up of newer and temporary accounts. As Reichheld explains, "It turned out that route drivers learned valuable shortcuts when their customer books were stable."

Reichheld also describes a catalogue sales operation whose senior managers discovered, through careful cost analysis, that the cost of processing orders for customers who had been with the company for less than two years was twice the cost of processing orders for longtime customers, for three reasons:

■ New customers, because they weren't familiar with the company's product line, were much more likely than longtime customers to ask for items the company didn't stock.

■ Credit evaluations and losses from new customers increased general overhead costs.

■ Newer customers tended to order at "peak-volume" times of the day, stressing the system and creating errors.

Reichheld uses these findings and other statistics to drive home a concept he refers to as the "life cycle profit pattern." The basic notion, as he explains it, is that it is possible—though not easy—to quantify the actual profit you derive from your customers based on how long you *retain* them as customers. He demonstrates with numerous graphs that the longer you hold on to a customer, the more profitable that customer becomes. The reasons he cites are as follows:

- *Spending patterns.* The spending patterns of loyal customers accelerate over time, particularly in companies that offer a variety of related products and services. In the automotive service industry, for instance, the average revenue generated per customer triples between the first and fifth year.

- *Less need for administrative and technical support.* Loyal customers are usually less expensive to support and service than new customers. Because they are familiar with what you carry or do, they do not depend as much as new customers on your employees for information and advice.

- *Customer referrals.* Loyal customers are a fruitful source of customer referrals; but more important is that they are a source of *quality* referrals. (Customers who have been referred to you by other customers are more likely than customers in general, according to Reichheld, to become loyal customers themselves, and to become, in effect, one of your sales reps.)

- *More margin for error.* Loyal customers—most of them, anyway—tend to be more tolerant of mistakes and, in fact, expect that problems will occur and will be worked out.

- *Lower likelihood for switching.* Loyal customers tend to resist switching. They view your company as a partner, and regard "doing business together" as a valued relationship. The one proviso: Their resistance can be overcome if there are significant differences between what

you offer in the way of features and what your competitors offer.

■ *Less fixation on price.* Loyal customers are not as fixated
on price as satisfied customers and, within reason, are
willing to accept and pay higher prices for premium
service or products because of the trust that has developed. It has been estimated, for example, that companies that enjoy high levels of customer loyalty are
able to charge, on average, about 10 percent more for
their basic products and services than competitors who
experience high customer turnover.

Reichheld presents one of the most compelling argu-
ments I've ever read on the pure economic advantages of
customer loyalty. And you don't need an MBA in finance to
appreciate the central message of that argument; namely,
that the financial health of your business, especially in the
long term, depends not only on the number of customers
you have and the revenues they are producing for you, but
on the length of time you are able to keep them in the fold.
With rare exceptions, the longer a customer has been
with you, the more profit you generate each time you make
a sale.

The implications of this principle are staggering. To
prove my point, take a moment or two to reflect on your
business. If your company is typical, the rate of customer
turnover is somewhere between 20 and 25 percent. But let's
assume, for the sake of argument, that you could figure out
a way to retain at least 5 percent of the customers you're
losing. I'm not talking here about all your customers, I'm
talking simply about 5 percent of the customers you're currently losing.

Do you have any idea what that 5 percent might mean to your bottom line? If you're in the software industry, your profitability would probably go up about 35 percent, everything else being equal. In the credit card industry, the profitability gain is closer to 75 percent. In bank deposits, it's even higher—85 percent.

Now let's look at some facts. In the banking industry today, surveys show that there's a fifty-fifty chance that the typical customer with a checking account will change banks at least once a year. Among those who have both a checking and a savings account, however, the odds are that the customer will defect will go up—to about 10 to 1. Add a safe deposit box to the mix, and the odds climb to about 20 to 1. And, if you have a customer who has checking and savings accounts, a safe deposit box, and a loan, the odds that the customer will defect climb to 100 to 1.

If you look at these odds within the context of profit patterns in banks, you can begin to appreciate the economics of retention. Most banks do not expect to make a profit on an account until the customer has been with the bank for 18 months. What does that tell you about the customers who leave after one year? Right, the banks lose money.

Think about this principle the next time you're tempted to blame the problems you are having with your business on shrinking profit margins. Your profit margins may indeed be shrinking, but if you were to look more closely, you might discover that, in addition to shrinking margins, what is really shrinking is something far more lethal: customer loyalty.

Chapter 2

❧❧❧❧

Looking for E-Gaps

An Inside Look at Customer Loyalty

I was an overnight guest not long ago at a major hotel where I was scheduled to deliver a speech. On the morning of the speech, I decided to have some breakfast in the hotel coffee shop, but because I had arrived late the night before and didn't check in until well after midnight, I didn't go down to the coffee shop until around 9:15, by which time most of the breakfast crowd had gone. But the coffee shop's official hours for breakfast, according to a sign in the lobby, were from 6:30 to 9:30, so I still had time—or so I thought.

I was wrong. To begin with, I had to stand at the entrance for two or three minutes before I could get anybody to even pay any attention to me. Finally, I was able to flag down one of the waitresses, who was clearing off some tables. She quickly informed me—the sign in the lobby notwithstanding—that it was too late to be "served" breakfast but that the buffet was still open.

Okay, I thought, I'll have the buffet, and within a few moments was eating one of the most singularly unappetizing breakfasts of my life. The scrambled eggs were cold. The muffins were like stones. And the fresh fruit simply wasn't. Worse, when I expressed my dissatisfaction—and very mildly!—to the waitress who had seated me, she suggested that I come to breakfast a little earlier.

Is It Deliberate?

Whenever I have one of these inexplicably unpleasant customer experiences, I can't help wondering if a group of people got together and *planned* it that way. How else to explain what happened? While I was finishing my cup of tea (make that tepid tea) that morning, for instance, I had an image of a meeting that might have taken place earlier that morning. I envisioned the hotel manager telling his food and beverage director, "John, we had some complaints about guests being greeted too promptly and courteously when they came into the coffee shop, particularly after 9:00. Can we do something about that—make them stand around cooling their heels for a while? And we also had problems with the eggs yesterday. They were fresh and hot; people thought they were tasty and really liked them. Let's not make that mistake again. It's our policy to serve eggs hard and cold."

I then heard in this imaginary meeting the hotel manager saying, "Barbara, about those muffins yesterday. They were much too fresh. Make sure you put them into the microwave for at least five minutes so that you can get them as hard as hockey pucks. And, by the way, the fruit was much too fresh. You know that our minimum is five days old."

Of course, no company goes out of its way to provide horrendous experiences for its customers. On the contrary, taking care of the needs of customers has become the management mantra of the 1990s. Virtually every major company in America within the past decade has instituted some variation of total quality management (TQM), and you would be hard-pressed to find any major company in almost any industry that hasn't developed mechanisms for tracking customer satisfaction and launched some form of internal campaign designed to improve customer satisfaction. Corporate leaders, in particular, have been unusually vocal on the subject—so much so that an IBM customer service specialist named Armen Kabodian recently gathered customer-service related comments from nearly 150 business leaders and put them together in a book called *The Customer Is Always Right* (McGraw-Hill, 1996).

Here's a brief sampling from that book. From William E. Butler of the Eaton Corporation, which manufactures vehicle components and electronic controls: "Our mandate today is to provide a level of quality that provides no less than customer delight." From Jim McCann, the president of 1-800 Flowers, Inc.: "What we need to create is nothing short of customer jubilation." From W. Randall Jones, the founder and CEO of Capital Publishing Company, Inc., publisher of *Worth* magazine: "Customer satisfaction is the oxygen of life at *Worth* magazine. In everything we do, customer satisfaction is Job One."

Clearly, what *isn't* lacking today in corporate America is an appreciation among corporate leaders of how important it is to take care of their customers, particularly when it comes to the basics. And it's clear, too, that most corporate leaders recognize that the old paradigm of customer satisfaction—being content with minimal levels of satisfaction—is no longer enough to keep customers loyal. As Thomas A. Stewart pointed out recently in *Fortune* ("After All You've Done for Your Customers, Why Are They Still Not Happy?" December 11, 1995), it is all but universally recognized today that customers are the defining element not just in individual businesses but in the economy as a whole. Says Stewart: "What matters most in an economy, in the final analysis, is how well an economy satisfies its customers' needs and wants."

Falling Short

But awareness and good intentions notwithstanding, the fact is that most companies today—major companies in particular—are falling considerably short of satisfying the basic needs and wants of their customers. According to the American Consumer Satisfaction Index (ACSI), a survey that was developed two years ago and is conducted annually by the University of Michigan and the American Society of Quality Control, the overall satisfaction level among American consumers in general is only slightly higher than 72 percent—a C-minus (*Fortune*, February 3, 1997).

More significant is that the trend is downward. The survey's most recent findings showed a 2 percent decline in satisfaction levels from the previous year, based on the responses from more than 30,000 users of some 3,900 products and services in more than two dozen industries and several public sector organizations, including the IRS. More importantly, of the 206 companies on the list, only

71 improved—and only 15 improved more than 4 percent. That levels of customer satisfaction are declining at the same time so many companies are on record as going out of their way to improve customer satisfaction is more than ironic. *Fortune*, in its analysis of the 1995 ACSI findings, took a look at the paradox and came up with three possible explanations; or, as *Fortune* put it, three "wrong turns" that business has made in general in its efforts to enhance customer satisfaction:

■ Viewing customer service as a "cost" and not an "investment."
■ Being insufficiently aware of the rising expectations of customers.
■ Failing to define customer satisfaction in a way that links it to financial results.

Whether *Fortune's* analysis is correct is debatable. What isn't debatable is the overall conclusion we can draw from the disparity between what companies are doing to enhance customer satisfaction and what is actually being achieved—that the current strategy isn't working. Each of the reasons *Fortune* cites factors in this phenomenon, but the overall reason can be expressed more succinctly: So few companies are realizing any success in their efforts to increase the satisfaction levels of their customers because not enough of these efforts are having an impact on the single most important factor in customer satisfaction: *the actual customer experience*, what customers go through when they buy, use, have questions about, or need to complain about the product or services they buy.

True, there are exceptions, and I'll be talking about the companies that exemplify these exceptions in later chapters. Overall, though, most companies that have launched major customer satisfaction initiatives have fallen into that classic big-company pitfall of looking for quick fixes. Lots of committees are being formed, surveys are being taken, videos are being produced, posters are being hung, and new positions ("relationship managers") are being created. All in all very little of such activity is having any impact on what is actually happening to customers in different phases of the customer experience. Worse, some strategies being adopted to enhance customer satisfaction are backfiring.

The computer industry, as *Fortune* points out, is a classic example of this. On the surface, most computer companies—especially the giants like IBM, Apple, and Compaq—would appear to be giving customers exactly what they want: better machines and software at lower costs. Yet satisfaction levels among computer users fell by nearly 3 percent between 1995 and 1996. And the most likely reason, according to *Fortune*, is that in their efforts to contain costs and prices, many companies have had to cut back on their customer service activities, at the same time they were going out of their way to attract new buyers—the very customers who need more hand-holding.

The computer industry is not the only industry "shooting itself in the foot" in this regard. Businesses in virtually every industry have succumbed over the years to the same pitfall: the failure to recognize the *totality* of the customer experience and the concomitant failure to allocate the time and the resources needed to ensure satisfaction in every aspect of this experience—particularly in the trenches. Typically, companies will spend millions of dollars developing ad campaigns designed to attract new customers by promising superior service but at the same time will do little or nothing to help front-line employees—the people responsible for delivering the service—follow through on that promise. A very powerful illustration of this comes to mind.

A 900-Pound Gorilla on the Phone

I was recently called in to meet with a major financial services institution to help it improve its image in the marketplace. Specifically, management said they wanted potential customers to view them as being "easy to do business with."

As part of my initial analysis I talked with some of their current "good" customers (who, it turned out, were far from satisfied). These customers complained that this company was not only difficult to deal with, but downright unpleasant. In fact, one customer described calling the company and "getting a 900-pound gorilla on the phone."

It got worse. On the day that I was to meet with the senior management team and report my initial findings, I saw, to my great surprise, full-page ads in the *Wall Street Journal* and the *New York Times* trumpeting the company's "improved customer service," complete with an 800 number listed in the suggestion to "Give us a call and experience the difference."

At the meeting, I pulled out the ad and asked them to help me understand the purpose of the campaign. I asked whether additional training had been given to the salespeople who staffed the 800 number? Did they issue guidelines to those who were dealing with customers? The director of marketing quickly jumped in and explained that there wasn't time for any of that; they had to do something about changing their image, and advertising was the best place to start. As it turned out, the people who were answering the phones (the same "900 pound gorillas") didn't even know the campaign was running!

It all came down to this: The company was quick to invest in splashy advertising, but reluctant to invest in the people who were actually delivering the service.

A Long-Term Commitment

The inescapable truth is this: Customer loyalty is not something you can create during brainstorming sessions with your ad agency. It isn't produced by catchy slogans or by high-sounding pronouncements in annual reports. And it isn't something you can generate in the short term, through one campaign.

Customer loyalty is something that builds on itself—the result of customers having extraordinary experiences at every point in their contact with your company. Every point. And if, as a company, you are not aware of all those contact points and how the experiences that customers have at each of these points affect overall customer satisfaction, your efforts to build customer loyalty—regardless of how much money, technology, or brainpower you pour into the effort—will fall short of your objective.

Building customer loyalty, in other words, must be a long-term strategy—highly focused, well-thought, carefully implemented and monitored. You can't create it in a fragmented, shotgun style, and it isn't enough to focus your service improvement efforts on one or two departments or functions. Everybody—everybody!—has to be part of the solution, otherwise they are part of the problem.

Is this initiative easy to pull off? Not in the least. And that's the problem. It is difficult enough to gear your business efforts to customer satisfaction alone. Raising the bar—seeking to produce complete satisfaction at every level of the buying experience—is doubling the challenge. You can't simply bundle a customer-loyalty initiative as an "add-on" to other goals and priorities. If your goal is to build a solid core of loyal customers, the strategy to reach that goal has to be organically tied to your company's basic business strategy. And you have to be prepared to make a sustained effort over a long period of time. Anything short of this commitment will doom the effort.

More Than Money

I wish I didn't have to paint so daunting a picture of what needs to be done to make the paradigm shift I'm advocating in this book. I would love to be able to offer you a handful of simple guidelines that you could institute in a matter of days and let the rest take care of itself. I can't.

It is worth emphasizing that the fundamental challenge you face when you commit yourself to creating customer loyalty instead of simple satisfaction isn't necessarily financial. As enumerated in later chapters, most of the steps you need to take to provide your customers with the kinds of exemplary experiences that build customer loyalty have much more to do with the way you think, plan, and operate than with the amount of money you're willing to spend. But however much money you choose to spend—assuming you spend it wisely—it is money that is likely to pay you back many times the original investment, bearing in mind the considerable financial benefits of employee loyalty. To repeat a point I made in the previous chapter, loyal customers are far friendlier to your bottom line than new customers.

E-Gaps and Intended Customer Experience

To help the businesses my company works with implement policies that do more than simply pay lip service to building customer loyalty, we've introduced two important concepts, both of which will figure prominently in what I have to say throughout the rest of this book. One of the concepts we call the E-*gap*. The other is something we call the *intended customer experience*.

E-Gap Defined

E-gap stands for *expectation gap*, and it is fairly self-explanatory: It is any gap that separates what customers expect when they do business with you and what they actually experience.

The premise behind the E-gap concept is that the subjective feeling customers normally experience as satisfaction or dissatisfaction is determined not only by what actually happens during any interaction between your company and your customers, but what the customers were expecting to happen. Any disparity between the expectation and the actual event is an E-gap. As such, E-gaps can work for you or against you. E-gaps work for you when the customer experience exceeds his or her expectations. They work against you when the customer's experience falls short of expectations. To express the same thought another way, positive E-gaps promote customer loyalty; negative E-gaps erode customer loyalty.

A Closer Look at E-Gaps

Conceptually, the E-gap is not new. It is simply a different way of looking at how you treat your customers. More specifically, it is a way of verifying whether the strategies and policies you are implementing in your efforts to satisfy your customers are producing the desired results. Analyzing your customer service efforts in terms of E-gaps forces you to do something you don't necessarily do when evaluating customer service: You focus on specifics. E-gaps enable you to see more clearly than you might otherwise that each interaction your customers have with your product or service carries with it the potential for an E-gap, either positive or negative, which, in turn, will influence the level of overall satisfaction the customers experience and the loyalty you are likely to instill.

We spend a great deal of time in our workshops and seminars teaching managers to look at their businesses and, in particular, their customer service initiatives in terms of E-gaps, those specific points along the customer-company continuum where companies are—or aren't—meeting customer expectations. And we find it to be an unusually powerful method. The concept alone enables senior managers, often for the first time, to "get it," to recognize why, in the face of everything the company is doing to make customers happy, customer satisfaction surveys consistently fail to record any improvement. Managers realize, for example, that what they might consider to be a "little thing"—navigating a labyrinth of voice mail connections to get a problem solved—can be a "big thing" to a customer who needs help in a hurry. Managers realize, too, that customer expectations are constantly changing, and are often shaped by factors over which they have little or no control, such as what their competitors are offering.

One point we emphasize about E-gaps is that the expectations on which they are based are highly relative. The following anecdote will illustrate what I mean by relative:

> At a party, I heard somebody exclaiming—yes, exclaiming—about the experience he'd had earlier that day in, of all places, the Motor Vehicle Bureau. Since none of the experiences I've had at the Motor Vehicle Bureau are worth bragging about, I was curious.
>
> "A guy came up to me as soon as I walked in" said the man. "He gave me a cheerful hello, and asked me what I needed to do, and told me what forms I had to fill out, and where to stand in line. He even came over as I was filling out the forms and asked me if I needed any help. It was terrific."
>
> "Terrific?" I asked.
>
> "Sure," the man said. "The last time I went to the Motor Vehicle Bureau, I had no idea of what to do or where to go, and I ended up spending 20 minutes in the wrong line."

This story illustrates how little it takes in certain situations to produce a positive E-gap. The challenge in this particular example, however, is that the next time this fellow goes to the Motor Vehicle Bureau, he will be expecting a certain type of experience. If that expectation is not met—you guessed it—a negative E-gap.

Herein lies a partial explanation for why the satisfaction levels in certain industries are lagging despite initiatives designed specifically to increase satisfaction. "What makes customer satisfaction so difficult to achieve," says Gun Dukes, a group director in the research department of J.D. Power & Associates, "is that you constantly raise the bar and extend the finish line. You never stop. As your customers get better treatment, they demand better treatment."

Making E-Gaps Work for You

I have much more to say in later chapters about E-gaps and how you can put the concept to work in your efforts to build customer loyalty in your company. But first, let me introduce and describe a companion concept, something we call the *intended customer experience.*

Like the E-gap, the intended customer experience is easy to define: It's what you want your customers to think, feel, and do whenever they interact in any way with your company. Envisioning the intended customer experience vastly increases your ability to identify potential E-gaps.

Dr. Murray Klauber, chairman and owner of the Colony Beach and Tennis Resort in Sarasota, Florida, is a former orthodontist who has become one of Florida's most successful real estate developers, even though he wasn't formally trained in the business. He credits his success to what can best be described as his diligent use of the intended customer experience concept. What he does can be applied to any business.

Klauber says that whenever he is thinking about any aspect of his business, he tries to give himself a "big chunk of quiet time, and he walks himself through every element of the customer experience." He has a notebook filled with notes he has taken whenever he has traveled. The notebook, he says, contains "all the little things that have happened that have delighted me and all the little things that have happened that made me upset, and I incorporate those experiences in my planning." He takes nothing for granted—not even something as routine as what happens when a guest calls room service. "If I'm working with a designer on a hotel room, I'll ask the designer, 'Okay, I've just walked into the door of my room, what's the first thing that hits me in the eye? Or, I'm going to be hanging up my clothes in the closet. How easy is it going to be for me to do this?'"

Does this seem like overkill to you? Perhaps. Yet I'm willing to bet that if the computer industry managers who made the decision to cut back on customer support services at the same time they were lowering their prices and attracting new customers had set aside some quiet time and imagined how they would feel the first time they called customer support and had to stay on hold for 45 minutes, they wouldn't have been the least bit surprised at the results of the ACSI survey. They would have seen quickly that by cutting back on customer support they were practically guaranteeing a negative E-gap. I suspect, too, that the hotel experience I described to you at the beginning of this chapter, while it may not have been deliberately scripted, was, nonetheless, made more likely by one or more management decisions. It might have had to do with saving money on staffing or on equipment. I don't know; but I do know that it created a negative E-gap of immense proportions.

I should point out here that these two concepts—E-gaps and the intended customer experience—are not, in and of themselves, the ultimate solution for whatever might be wrong with your business. As a business owner myself, I don't need to be reminded about the basics of business economics. And as useful and as powerful a tool as the intended customer experience exercise can be, I have to maintain perspective. It may not be possible for any number of reasons to provide your customers with the perfect experience you envision when you go through this exercise. But that's not the real point of the exercise. The point is to expand your awareness, to focus your attention and your efforts on areas of your business that you might be ignoring and that could have greater impact on your success than you think.

I also suspect that key decision makers in the domestic automobile industry went through an exercise very much like the one I've been describing; that is, they sat down and started to focus on all the various points along the line where their customers were having interactions that might affect their satisfaction. And at one point, it might have occurred to them that most of these interactions take place *after* the car has been purchased—when the customer takes in the car for servicing. Somebody, either intuitively or consciously, must have put him- or herself in the shoes of a car owner and asked, "What sort of an experience would I like to have when I go to get my car serviced at this dealership?" How else to explain the discernible and dramatic change in the procedure at the most successful dealerships today when you bring in your car for servicing: the coffee and bagels that await you in the lounge, the loaner car you're given, that your car comes back to you not only serviced but washed and vacuumed—all at no extra charge. I'm told that Saturn dealerships place a tasty piece of chocolate candy on the dashboard or flowers on the front seat as a way of saying "thanks for bringing your car into Saturn." Some Infiniti dealerships have gone even further, offering free massages to regular customers.

How costly are these little extras? A bare fraction, I would suggest, of what the automobile companies pay for advertising and other marketing expenses. The only real cost is time and effort—and that's not a cost, really, but an investment. Sure, American car companies may be turning out better cars these days, but I don't believe that it's purely coincidental that customer satisfaction levels are increasing at the same dealerships that are going out of their way to take care of their customers even after the purchase. Whether they realize it, successful dealerships are creating positive E-gaps, and, in the process, they're building something that all the horsepower in the world can't generate: customer loyalty.

Chapter 3

─────────── ❦ ❦ ❦ ❦ ───────────

Customer Loyalty

The Employee Connection

A friend of mine recently came back from a business trip to Pittsburgh with the following story. She was staying in a hotel on the outskirts of the city and had rented a car, but she wasn't sure how to get to the offices of the company she was scheduled to visit. So on the morning of the appointment, she went to the front desk and asked the young woman working behind the counter for directions. The reception clerk said she had a general idea of where the company was located but didn't feel comfortable giving directions. But she didn't stop there. She went into the back office and summoned one of the night clerks who, as it turned out, was on his way home and lived not far from where my friend needed to go. "I could draw a rough map for you," the clerk said, "but it's tricky. So the best thing would be to follow me. You don't have to worry; I'll make sure you get there."

"What bowled me over," my friend said, "is how concerned everybody at the front was with the little problem that I had. What a great hotel."

What we have here, of course, is a classic example of one of those customer interactions that exceeds customer expectations, produces a positive E-gap, and, eventually, results in customer loyalty. That's obvious. Less obvious is how you as an owner or manager set the stage for such experiences. I've seen dozens of procedures manuals for the hospitality industry, but I can't recall ever reading a policy that obliges employees who are asked to give directions to personally escort guests to their destinations.

Experiences like the one I've just described cannot be programmed, strictly speaking, into your business operation. The night clerk didn't *have* to go to the trouble of making sure my friend got to her appointment on time. He did so out of choice. It was a discretionary act performed by an employee who obviously felt a strong obligation to look after the welfare of the hotel's customers. It takes a special kind of employee to feel that sense of obligation, and it takes a special kind of company to create the environment that attracts, retains, and motivates employees to perform these actions.

The Power of Discretionary Effort

We've conducted a good deal of informal research among employees in a variety of companies, and have found that, generally speaking, most employees—particularly lower- and middle-level employees who deal directly with customers—can meet the basic requirements of their jobs with somewhere in the neighborhood of 60 percent of their total attention and commitment.

These employees aren't slacking off when they put only 60 percent of their effort into their jobs; in most instances, it's simply that the jobs can be adequately performed most of the time with routine, by-the-numbers, automatic-pilot type effort. If you are a receptionist (in companies that still use receptionists instead of elaborate voice-mail systems), you can work a crossword puzzle or compose sonnets at the same time you're answering the phone and directing callers to their appropriate parties. If you drive your company's delivery truck, you don't really need to know what business the customer is in or what sort of pressures the customer is typically under; all you need to know, really, is the customer's address and how many cartons need to be unloaded. If you book airline reservations by phone, you don't need to know—or care—why the customer needs to get somewhere or what sort of budget the customer is on; all you need to know is where the customer wants to go and which flights go there at what time. If you're a clerk in a retail computer store, you don't have to be concerned with how easy or difficult it's going to be for a customer to set up the computer—not if there's an 800-customer support number.

In some businesses—depending upon the product or service you sell or the marketplace you're in—you can be reasonably successful with employees who simply "do their jobs." But as you should appreciate by now, minimal business-as-usual efforts do not produce the exemplary experiences that result in customer loyalty. Customer loyalty can be won only when employees consistently tap into that 40 percent of discretionary effort, when they understand in their bones that their ultimate job, indeed the ultimate job of everybody in your organization, is to look after the welfare of the customer.

The exact nature of that 40 percent discretionary effort is, however, difficult to isolate, except to say that it always extends beyond the normal parameters of any particular job description or function. And yet, when you are the beneficiary of it as a customer, you notice it and you remember it. You notice it when a receptionist you've reached doesn't just say to you, "I'm sorry, we have no one here by that name," but takes a genuine interest in your problem and goes out of his or her way to direct you to the right person. You notice it when the airline reservations clerk says to you, "That flight is completely booked, but let me see if I can figure out a way to get you where you want to go." You notice it when the person who delivers the merchandise from one of your suppliers doesn't dump a load of cartons on your doorstep but goes out of the way to make sure that the boxes go where you want them, never mind that it's 95 degrees outside and it takes an extra 10 minutes. You notice it when the clerk who has sold you a computer says, "You shouldn't have any trouble setting up, but just in case you do, here's my home phone."

Of course, in and of themselves, these added efforts—discretionary or otherwise—can't compensate for any failure to deliver on the basics. As impressed and grateful as my friend was with the concern demonstrated by the desk clerks at the hotel she stayed at, she wouldn't go back there if the room had been unclean or if she could have gotten a comparable room nearby for half the price. So I don't want to overstate the case for discretionary effort and its impact on customer loyalty, but it is important to factor it in when you are evaluating customer service practices in your business.

Inspiring the Attitudes That Produce Customer Loyalty

No company can expect to build customer loyalty unless the employees who interact with customers are willing and able to put forth the discretionary effort that underlies exemplary customer experiences. Simply put, if you want your customers to be loyal, you must instill in your employees the appropriate attitudes so they are willing to make the commitment, not here or there in your organization but *throughout*. It's up to you to motivate those attitudes and that commitment; there is no other way, not in today's competitive marketplace. Unless you're a one-person band—the only person in your organization whose activities have any impact on the customer experience—you can't generate customer loyalty yourself, and for the most obvious of reasons: You cannot be personally involved in every interaction that has the potential to produce a negative E-gap. You cannot answer every phone call, deliver every package, handle every inquiry. You need employees who are (or should be) as dedicated as you are to creating value for your customers. To express the same thought another way, if you want loyal customers, you need loyal employees—and you need to make sure that you are giving those employees the support and the guidance they need to put that loyalty to work where it counts the most: taking care of the customer.

Defining Employee Loyalty

We know what loyal customers are: They're the customers who keep coming back to you not because they have no other options but because they value those qualities that differentiate you from your competitors. They are also the customers who do the most for your company's bottom line, for all the reasons I've cited in earlier chapters.

But what do we mean when we talk about "loyal employees?" What qualities differentiate loyal employees, and what do these qualities mean to your business? The answer to these questions are not as obvious as you may think. Loyalty is a tricky word to define when it comes to employees. Some employees would describe themselves as loyal simply because they're trustworthy—they can be counted upon to show up for work every day, and they do what they're asked to do. But the kind of loyalty I'm talking about here goes beyond these basic, though admirable, qualities. The kind of loyalty I'm talking about springs from an attitude that elicits from employees that added extra 40 percent of discretionary effort that can often mean the difference between a customer who is merely satisfied and a customer who is completely satisfied.

It is, of course, the basic argument of this book that customer loyalty and employee loyalty are inextricably linked. The abstract nature of these terms makes it difficult to prove empirically that such a link exists, but there is a preponderance of indirect evidence. The most striking is the correlation between customer retention and employee retention. It doesn't matter what industry you analyze, the pattern is almost invariably the same: the higher the rate of customer satisfaction, the lower the rate of employee turnover.

Studies in the brokerage industry, for instance, have found that customers who have to deal with two or more brokers are 33 percent more likely to defect than customers who work with only one broker. The nation's most profitable brokerage firm, A.G. Edwards, ranks number one in both customer retention and employee retention, yet spends almost nothing on national advertising and deliberately shuns many of the motivational practices— multitiered commission systems, for instance—employed by other firms.

There is striking evidence, too, from the fast-food industry—an industry that accepts high employee turnover as a given—that if you can reduce turnover, you can increase both volume and profitability. And when Bain & Co. analyzed the auto service business, it found that the highest rates of customer loyalty were found among that segment of the business—local garages—that also enjoyed the highest rate of employee retention. This is a logical pattern but one that requires an interesting footnote: Bain found that although most people believed that mechanics at chain outlets and auto dealers were better trained and had more sophisticated equipment than local mechanics, they had more faith in the judgment of their local mechanics. Frederick Reichheld explains, "People simply felt more comfortable doing repeat business with the same individual, regardless of technical finesse. They stayed with local mechanics because they knew them and because they knew their cars. At the larger outlets, customers rarely saw the mechanic twice."

Employee Loyalty in Today's Workplace

If you are like the business professionals I lecture to or work with in my seminars, I have a rough idea of what you are thinking right now. You're probably willing to accept—because the evidence is so overwhelming—that building customer loyalty is not only a worthwhile goal but an *essential* goal in today's marketplace. I would hope, too, that by now you recognize that everybody in your organization, from top to bottom, has to be committed to that goal.

It's likely, though, that something else is going through your mind. You are probably wondering whether I'm aware of what is going on today in workplaces throughout the United States, whether I have gotten the message that employee loyalty is a thing of the past, as out of sync with today's times as the manual typewriter.

I have indeed gotten the message—loud and clear. Having been involved in corporate life for more than two decades, I'm familiar with the trend in companies throughout the United States, and in particular, with the unsettling mood that now permeates the workplace, especially in those major corporations that have experienced wrenching downsizings.

It's not a pretty picture, by any means. According to a *New York Times* poll conducted in conjunction with a seven-part series ("The Downsizing of America") that ran early in 1996, American employees overall are more concerned about job security and are more distrustful of the companies they work for than at any other period since the Great Depression. Seventy-five percent of American workers now view the companies they work for as being *less* loyal than companies were 10 years ago; and 65 percent of American workers believe that workers themselves are less loyal than they were 10 years ago. Further, the percentage of American workers who describe their workplaces as "angrier" places to work compared to the way things used to be is six times greater than the percentage of American workers who describe their workplaces as "friendlier."

Disquieting as they are, these statistics are hardly surprising, not when you consider all the turmoil and pain that have resulted from the massive layoffs, restructurings, and downsizings that have taken place, to one degree or another, in almost every major corporation in America. Periodic job reductions have always been a fact of life for certain segments of the workplace—blue collar workers, in particular. The difference now, however, is that layoffs hit professionals who historically never had to be concerned with job security—college-educated administrative and middle management personnel in large corporations. And while it is true that the number of jobs in America over the past 25 years has increased, the past 15 years have marked the first time that major companies instituted large-scale layoffs as *permanent* policy and not simply as a temporary response to a slowdown in the economy. True, the vast majority of people who have been victims of these unprecedented cutbacks have managed to find new jobs, but only one-third of them, according to the U.S. Department of Labor Statistics, have found replacement jobs with comparable salaries, benefits, and stature. Little wonder that when the New York Times asked its survey respondents if they thought today's youth would have a "better life" than their parents, nearly 50 percent responded that this prospect was either "somewhat unlikely" or "very unlikely."

It is too early to tell just how necessary all this corporate bloodletting really was. Clearly, there was a need for major corporations to reengineer themselves in light of the pressures of global competition. Without question, many major corporations had become far too bureaucratic and too bloated around the middle. Moral implications aside, they could no longer afford the luxury of paying salaries and benefits to employees whose functions were no longer having a direct impact on the bottom line. As Noel Tichy and Stratford Sherman point out in *Control Your Destiny or Someone Else Will* (Doubleday, 1993), a book that charts the reengineering of General Electric (GE), the highly structured, bureaucratic structure that served major corporations well from the end of World War II through the mid-1970s had become an albatross. Like other corporate giants, GE, according to Tichy and Sherman, was burdened with a corporate culture that had started to "strangle the business."

GE, according to this book, was choking on a nit-picking system of formal reviews and approvals, which delayed decision, thwarted common sense, and often made the company a laggard at bringing new products to market. For executives, a mastery of arduous procedures had become an art form, almost an unspoken requirement for advancement. The result: Many of GE's best managers devoted far more energy to internal matters than to their customers' needs.

I spent the early part of my career working for two corporations that epitomized what Tichy and Sherman have to say about GE, and so I have no trouble accepting the validity of their analysis. But more often, as I work closely with companies that have instituted massive restructurings and layoffs to reegineer their cultures, I see firsthand the bitter harvest of downsizing. And I have little doubt that whatever it may have accomplished, downsizing in and of itself—particularly in the way it has been handled in most major corporations—is far from the ultimate right to what is wrong.

And I'm not talking here about the *personal* effects of downsizing—that is, the incalculable psychological toll on the millions of people who have lost jobs or are members of a household that has been hit by a job loss. I'm talking more in pure business terms, whether downsizing has achieved the bottom-line results it was supposed to bring about. In the short term, yes, downsizing did help most companies solve at least one problem: It produced the kind of bottom-line blip on which Wall Street analysts tend to base their "buy" recommendations; as such, it tended to make stockholders happy, although not for very long. When the *Wall Street Journal*, in 1993, took a close look at firms that had undergone significant downsizings within the previous five years, it found that fewer than half of these companies had actually increased their profits, and that only a third were reporting higher productivity. The same analysis showed that while share prices of companies undergoing downsizing had enjoyed a brief spike during the six months following the news of downsizing or restructuring, the net performance of these companies after a three-year period, measured against the S&P 500, was nearly 25 percent less than the S&P 500.

But, let's be fair. The fact that downsizing was not enough to resuscitate the fortunes of ailing companies that opted for this radical strategy does not necessarily mean that the companies would be better off today if they hadn't eliminated so many jobs. But these numbers certainly oblige us to question the wisdom of the strategy itself, and the way it is usually implemented.

Based on what I have observed over the past several years, for far too many corporations downsizing became the silver bullet, the quick fix, the one bold stroke that was ostensibly meant to make up for the complacency and the misguided policies that had put many of these companies in jeopardy to begin with. What happened time and again is that companies buckling under competitive pressure began chopping away at their employee population without giving sufficient thought to what really needed to be done in order to regain their competitive edge. And most companies, even those that did their best to take care of the employees being let go, failed to appreciate sufficiently the impact the downsizings would have, not only on the people who lost their jobs but on the "survivors," and in many cases, on customers. "We were definitely guilty of this reaction," admits Dan Wiljanen, vice president of corporate human resources for Steelcase, reflecting on the downsizing that his company went through in August 1991. "It was traumatic for everybody—not just for the people who lost their jobs."

Steelcase, fortunately, is one of a handful of companies that learned from its early mistakes. Since that first downsizing, the company has experienced two or three difficult periods but has responded to these challenges in a much more measured manner. "What we learned from all of this," says Wiljanen, "is that periodically there are going to be inevitable business cycles, and that the best thing to do overall is to try to tough it out. The better long-term approach |to the earlier difficulty| would have been to try to tough it out during that period—to do what we could do in terms of reemploying people, or make use of that downtime for training."

Steelcase is not the only company that has taken a second look at downsizing as the response to a more competitive marketplace. When Harmen Karden, the audio speaker company, experienced a market dip recently, for instance, it didn't immediately cut staff. Instead, the company gathered its employees into small groups and put into place a campaign designed to reduce costs in ways that didn't necessarily require employees be let go. As I will show in later chapters, companies that have looked for alternatives to downsizing to enhance their competitive edge are being repaid by enhanced employee performance. In contrast, companies that haven't learned from their mistakes are paying a high price in the form of something I call a *loyalty-deficit cycle.*

Chapter 4

꙳ ꙳ ꙳ ꙳

The Loyalty-Deficit Cycle

Any company in which employee loyalty is on decline is suffering from a *loyalty-deficit cycle*. And companies seeking to build customer loyalty while trapped in this cycle are between the proverbial rock and a hard place. The harder they push their employees to take batter care of customers, the less likely most employees are to put forth the discretionary effort that represents the difference between satisfying customers and providing customers with the kinds of experiences that build loyalty.

Companies caught in this cycle are not difficult to recognize. For one thing, they tend to institute a lot of rules. For another, they go out of their way to replace employee effort with technology. Let's take a closer look at each of these misguided strategies and why they rarely produce the results that companies want.

Loyalty by the Rule Book

A surprising number of decision makers in companies are operating under the assumption that the best way to ensure superior customer service is to formulate and enforce an extensive set of procedures and policies that cover virtually every situation that might arise.

There's an easy way to identify such companies. Take a look at their employee manual, and if you have trouble lifting it with one hand, you can be sure that you're dealing with a rule-bound company. You can also be reasonably sure that what you're *not* going to find in these companies is a growing number of loyal customers.

No company can function efficiently without rules, but you have to know when you've reached the breaking point. Being too rule-bound in your approach to customer service stifles the very impulses in employees that produce discretionary effort. Rules, by definition, are designed to ensure *compulsory* effort, not encourage discretionary effort. Usually, you can count on the 60 percent baseline effort from employees, but you rarely get the additional 40 percent discretionary effort. Rules often cause a conflict between what a committed employee might be normally *inclined* to do and what the rule book dictates.

An even more significant problem in rule-bound organizations is that much time and effort must be expended to make sure the rules are being followed. We've all heard the same message whenever we've had occasion to call an insurance or credit card company. A recorded voice informs us that "for quality purposes, the call may be monitored." To me this means the company doesn't trust its employees. I can only imagine what employees infer from this policy.

The alternative, which we'll look at more closely in a later chapter, is to create a system that gives employees a clear set of guidelines while allowing them a certain amount of discretion when dealing with customers. A good example is the New York restaurant company Cafe Concepts, whose flagship restaurant, Trattoria Dellarte generates yearly revenues that rank it among the top 20 of all independent restaurants across the United States. The service procedures manual at the five restaurants that comprise this company consists of only a handful of pages, because the restaurants accord their waiters and waitresses far more autonomy than you find in most similar companies.

"We have a philosophy, not rules," says Sheldon Fireman, Cafe Concepts founder and president. "The philosophy is to treat the guests in our restaurants as if they were guests in our own home." Fireman goes on to explain that when a guest doesn't seem to be enjoying a particular dish, his waiters and waitresses don't wait for a complaint. They go quickly to the table to find out if there is something else they can get for the guest. And if a guest has any problem with the dish, it's up to each waiter—not the people in the kitchen—to decide whether the person should get another selection. Waiters have the discretion, too, if they think it's appropriate, to do something extra for a table—maybe bring an after-dinner drink. "When people understand and believe in the philosophy," Fireman says, "you don't need a lot of rules."

A Machine to Fix It

Technological advances have had an enormous impact on the way customers interact with their companies, but the impact hasn't always worked to the benefit of either party.

Let's start with the upside. Technological advances have enabled manufacturing companies to improve the quality of their products, and service companies to broaden and speed up their services, providing customer conveniences that were never before possible. Thanks to technology, you no longer have to confine your banking activities from 9:00 A.M. to 3:00 P.M. And thanks to technology, you no longer have to worry about losing your airplane ticket; you make your reservations, submit your credit card number, and go right to the gate.

For many companies, however, technology has become an instrument whose principal function is not so much to serve the needs of the customer but to save money and to control employees. In our local supermarket not long ago, for example, I began to notice one particular cashier who not only was able to scan groceries very quickly, but also managed to bag them—something the others didn't seem to be doing. So, one day, I deliberately got into her aisle to try and figure out how she was able to accomplish this feat. I saw that she would scan a few items and then hit a key on the register, scan a few more items, hit the register key, and so on. Finally, unable to get the connection, I asked her, "Why do you keep reaching over to hit that key on the register?" She laughed and said, "Oh, it's really very simple," and as she continued working, she explained that performance in this supermarket was measured by how long it took them to check out customers. "Each register has a timer and the timer starts with the first scan," she told me. "The times go into a report that consolidates all of our weekly customer activity, and we're told just how long it should take us to get customers through, based on the size of the bill."

She then confided to me that she'd made an interesting discovery. She found that when she hit the subtotal key, it turned off the timer, so she could take the time to scan the groceries and bag them without being penalized.

This is a good example, I think, of an organization trying to control by technology: being efficient yet defeating its own goal of providing better service to customers.

I found another example of technology being used for what I consider misguided purposes in a series of magazine ads promoting a new software program whose purpose is to closely track the activities of a company's sales force. "Imagine knowing for sure where your salespeople really go," is how the ad begins—the implication being that salespeople cannot be trusted. Some salespeople do indeed "goof off" on the job, but if I were working for a company that, on the one hand, was telling me to be "consultative," and to build "partnerships" with my customers, but on the other hand, was installing a Big Brother-type software program designed to keep tabs on where I was at every moment of the day, I don't think I'd be in the frame of mind that would encourage customer loyalty.

These two approaches, rules and technology, are hardly new. The efficiency-based method they epitomize took root in the 1920s. Known as "scientific management," its premise was to control work productivity through time-and-motion studies. One of the great perceived "benefits" of this approach was to make manufacturing processes "peopleproof."

Such an approach may have indeed produced some productivity gains, but remember that this paradigm was originally intended to apply to manufacturing—to control people and processes that didn't involve direct customer contact. In today's economy, something like 80 percent of

companies are in service businesses, and it is questionable whether these gains in productivity ultimately translate into a service company's ability to generate long-term
profitability. Controlling people and processes by technology does not necessarily result in an experience that exceeds customers expectations and give them a reason to
come back.

The Salary Factor

When technology rules, wages tend to drop. Equipment
is often purchased because it ostensibly enables companies to hire employees who are less skilled and therefore less expensive. Tasks that were once the province of
human judgment become automated, which means you
no longer need people who have the skill and the sensitiv-
ity to make decisions. The process becomes more important than the people who run it. People can be replaced;
the process can't.

What happens? Companies caught up in the notion that
machines are more cost-effective than people (all things
being equal) do not spend a lot of time or thought on the
employee selection process. Instead, the idea is to find a
warm body—preferably one that will work for the minimum
wage. This being the case—a low-paid employee hired to
perform a limited function—there isn't much point in providing a lot of training. Minimal training moves employees
and the organization further along the deficit cycle, to a
point where employees feel a low sense of competence
about their capabilities.

Here again, though, is an approach to business that, on
the surface, has a strong economic rationale. But what you

see is not necessarily what you get. The more you try to eliminate the human factor from job functions—to make these functions "peopleproof"—the more interchangeable and dehumanized the employees become. It's almost impossible, in fact, for employees to feel any sense of self-worth or competency when they work in systems that have been designed to minimize their contribution. Employees thus become dissatisfied in their jobs, not only because of the lack of recognition and rewards for any abilities they may possess or because they are boxed into jobs with no opportunity to apply or develop those abilities further, but also because they are not allowed to provide customers with very good service.

Don't underestimate the impact that the job satisfaction rate among your employees has on the satisfaction level of your customers. Most job satisfaction surveys report that the number one criterion among employees who deal directly with customers is the sense of being able to help the customer solve a problem. Without the right skills, the right tools, the right orientation, and the right compensation, employees have no recourse but to feel powerless and dissatisfied.

The one factor we know about dissatisfied employees is that, given other options, they'll leave you in a moment. That's why organizations in a loyalty-deficit cycle almost invariably suffer high turnover. That means the organization is denying itself the training and knowledge it needs to better serve customers. High turnover also means that employees don't learn and thus can't pass on what they've learned from dealing with customers in a variety of situations. So, an organization of this type is usually characterized by poor service delivery and lower profitability.

The connection between high turnover and reduced profitability is indisputable. But companies in this cycle frequently overlook exactly how much employee turnover is costing them in actual dollars. As with customers, it costs much more to lose and replace an employee than to keep one (benefits included). Several studies have indicated that, over a seven-year period ending in 1992, the average cost of losing and replacing an hourly worker was anywhere from $5,000 to $10,000; replacing a middle manager can cost a company one and a half times that person's salary; and replacing an executive with an annual salary of $100,000 can range from $75,000 to $210,000. Perry Christensen, former director of work/life programs at Merck Pharmaceutical, estimates that the cost of replacing an exempt employee is 1.5 times the annual salary for that position; for a nonexempt employee, it's three-quarters of the annual salary. Jerry Florence from Nissan Motor Company takes those numbers higher, ballparking the cost of hiring, training, developing, increasing and expanding the skills of a Nissan employee at $1 million. "Therefore," he says, "losing one employee costs that much, or constitutes a loss to the company, minus whatever productivity was achieved during the period of employment."

Which brings us to the final wrinkle in the loyalty-deficit cycle: the ultimate reduction in profitability, and the predictable response. Companies experiencing bottom-line problems tend to repeat the steps that got them into the cycle in the first place. Faced with decreasing profits, they retrench. They tighten rules still further, put more controls in place, hire more expendable warm bodies, pay lower wages . . . until it's all spinning out of control.

Chapter 5

———— ❧❧ ❧❧ ❧❧ ❧❧ ————

Breaking the
Loyalty-Deficit Cycle

We have spent a great deal of time in our company working with organizations that are struggling to overcome the corrosive effects of the loyalty-deficit cycle. One of the by-products of this experience is that I have emerged with an unusual kind of expertise: I am uniquely qualified to offer surefire advice on what you should—and shouldn't—do in your company if you are determined to kill all hope of creating employee loyalty. Tongue in cheek, I frequently share this "expertise" during my lectures. And I'm going to take this opportunity to share this knowledge with you. You might call this advice the Seven Steps to Guarantee Failure in today's competitive environment.

1. *Don't put any thought into your hiring procedures.* The first—and, in some ways, the most fundamental—step to

follow if you're truly committed to perpetuating a loyalty-deficit cycle is to pay as little attention as possible to your hiring procedures. In other words, don't take the time to analyze your business needs so that you can determine—*before* you place an ad in the local paper—what specific mixture of skills and qualifications are needed to perform a particular task at the highest level in your company. Don't bother to put yourself into your customers' shoes to figure out where all the E-gaps are. Doing so might force you to use customer needs as the chief criteria of your hiring philosophy and policies, and endanger your chances of hiring the "wrong" person. And don't waste your time trying to figure out what type of employee might be best suited to those criteria. Go the "warm body" route. Do whatever is the easiest and most expedient.

While you're at it, don't put any thought into your recruiting procedures. Do what is the most expedient and the cheapest: a hurriedly written newspaper ad, or a notice on the bulletin board of your local supermarket. And when letters and resumes start to pour in, be sure you delegate the task of selecting the best candidate to whomever has a lot of experience evaluating job candidates and matching skills and attributes to your business needs—perhaps the guy who runs your company's cleaning service. Employees, remember, are interchangeable: If one doesn't work out, you can always find a replacement, especially at the lower levels.

2. *Keep salary and benefits costs as low as possible.* Since salaries and benefits to your employees are direct "expenses"—they go straight to the bottom line—try to get away with paying your employees as little as possible, regardless of their needs and the market value of the job. Let the spendthrifts

out there waste their money on salaries that might actually attract and keep the best people. And be particularly parsimonious when it comes to benefits or any other expenditures that might make your company a more pleasant or interesting place to work. You're running a company, remember, not a country club or a social agency. If employees complain about conditions, or make unreasonable requests, such as asking to take time off to take a sick child to the doctor, or for soap in the restrooms or a small refrigerator so that they don't have to spend half their salary on lunches, remind them that you're not a social agency or a restaurant. You run a *business*, and you have to remain competitive. The more money you waste on "perks" for your employees, the more pressure you put on your bottom line.

3. *Run a tight ship*. If low motivation and high turnover are your goals, don't be sucked in by all the talk you hear these days about "participatory management," "empowerment," and "team-building." These trends are nothing but ivory tower notions that end up causing much more grief than they're worth. Everybody knows that most employees just want to put in their 9 to 5, and then hightail it back home so that they can flop on the couch, eat a pizza, and pop open a can of beer. Treat your employees like children; they like that. Employees are happiest when you tell them what to do and don't put any pressure on them to apply their own intelligence, ingenuity, or creativity to their jobs

More specifically, institute lots of rules, and don't worry if the rules have nothing to do, really, with how effectively the work is done or how successfully your employees are exceeding the expectations of your customers. It's much more important to keep things predictable and orderly in your company than to create value for your customers. It's okay to have a suggestion box, but don't get carried away. What do employees know, anyway? Most of the ideas they come up with will end up costing you a lot of money. And don't bother to orient new people, either. Just hand them the nine-pound policy manual you've developed, and make sure they read it and understand how you "do things around here."

4. *Don't waste money on training.* Training would be an acceptable idea except for three points: one, it costs money that you could otherwise use to build your home fitness center; two, it takes time; and, three, most of the employees you train end up leaving you anyway. So why bother?

There's an even bigger dilemma, though. If you train people, they're likely to start believing in themselves, and they might want to start to think—really think—about what they're doing and how they might do a better job of meeting the needs and exceeding the expectations of your customers. Just what you need, right? This impulse might actually force you to spend more time talking face to face with your employees, finding out from them what your customers are concerned about and how you might do a better job of meeting the needs of those customers.

One final note about the disadvantages of training. When people are trained, they tend to make fewer mistakes, which gives you fewer opportunities to criticize them. Train people, and before you know it, they'll start to feel competent and good about themselves; and the next thing you know, your customers will start to notice and will tell you how good a job your employees are doing, which, of course, will simply go to their heads and make them feel as though they're actually contributing something to the success of your organization. Now you're in real trouble.

5. *Manage by intimidation*. Assuming you have assembled a group of haphazardly chosen, poorly paid, and untrained employees, you need to figure out a way to light a fire under them so that you can overcome their inherent laziness. The best way to do this, by far, is through intimidation. Holler, scream, jump up and down, threaten, throw insults, single out people, embarrass them in public. Too bad we don't live in a true dictatorship. That way, you could hire armed guards to keep your employees on their toes.

Don't underestimate the value of these progressive management "tools." Intimidate people often enough and they'll never complain or bring to your attention any problems that might affect your customers. Why would you want to hear about problems? You have enough problems of your own, what with your golf handicap no lower than it was six months ago.

6. *Complain about turnover*. One of the benefits that will accrue to you—I guarantee it—if you follow the first five pieces of advice is that you will not have to endure the presence of most of the employees you hire for very long. Most will leave within a few months. When this happens, the best response is to not question your own policies but to brood and complain about the state of the world and the woeful condition of the nation's workforce. Share with your like-minded friends your conviction that the world is going to seed, and that you can't get good people anymore; ask why this new generation doesn't have the kind of work ethic that the previous generation did. Keep talking about the "good old days," even if you were too young to have actually experienced them.

7. *Be ready to lose customers*. The last piece of the puzzle that makes the loyalty-deficit cycle complete is to accept

that as long as you keep your employee turnover rate high, you're going to enjoy high customer turnover as well. It's a neat equation. At the same time you're losing employee loyalty, you're losing customer loyalty. Which really, when you think about it, makes life more interesting. It keeps you on your toes. And it makes it easier to defend your own job performance. With employees leaving, how can anyone expect you to keep your customers happy? And, then if you do what a lot of companies are doing today, you forget about retaining customers.

Back to Reality

It is no great challenge to pinpoint and satirize all the foolish things that companies do to discourage employee loyalty and to destroy all chances that their employees will deliver that extra discretionary effort that is the critical ingredient to promoting and preserving customer loyalty.

The true challenge is to offer solid and practical ideas that will serve as counterpoint to the "advice" I have just given you. Even in the best of times, when business is good and customers are happy, motivating the people who work for you to give that additional 40 percent of discretionary effort may be the single most difficult challenge in business. And as soon as things begin to go a little sour—competition increases, customers become more demanding, business starts to drop, and so on—the challenge becomes all the more daunting.

I have a lot to say throughout the rest of this book about how to go about meeting this challenge, and I will offer specific examples from companies that are doing so in a variety of ways. Bear in mind, though, that when discussing issues such as employee motivation and loyalty, there is the risk of making generalizations. Every business, large or small, is unique. And what works for you, given your business, your location, your community, your customers, may not work for somebody else. If you own a small business, you can be more flexible when it comes to handling the people aspect of your business than you could if you were the chairman and CEO of a multibillion dollar corporation—and, in particular, a multibillion dollar corporation whose shareholders are up in arms because your company's stock hasn't been keeping pace with the rest of the stock market. And if your company is financially healthy, you can do a lot more to motivate your employees than if you aren't sure there is enough money in the coffer to meet your next payroll. Remember, too, that what looks interesting and logical on paper doesn't always translate neatly to the reality of the daily functioning of your business. When it comes to putting into practice the ideas I will be sharing with you throughout the rest of this book, it isn't that the devil is in the details. The devil *is* the details.

And we have not even discussed the issue of *values*, which has to do more specifically with what obligations—if any—a company has to its employees other than to provide decent salaries and benefits, and a safe, humane working environment. There is an interesting and important debate going on throughout corporate America today, and it has to do with priorities: how companies should balance the needs and expectations of all their constituencies. In other words, who should take it on the chin when profit margins and earnings begin to drop: employees or stockholders? To whom do you listen, for example, when you're trying to decide whether to build an on-site child-care center: your director of human resources, who points out that 30 percent of your workforce is now composed of working mothers, or your chief accountant, who argues that the cost of building and running the center will take too big a bite out of the bottom line.

There is no right or wrong position in this debate. But what has been happening in recent years in response to a number of social and business trends is that even the most bottom line-oriented companies realize that they no longer have a choice: If they want to attract and keep good employees, they must pay at least some attention to the human needs of their employees. They now recognize that they cannot separate the pressures employees have to deal with at home from those at work. Nor can they assume, even in today's business environment, that simply because they're offering employees steady pay and reasonable benefits, that employees will be grateful and demonstrate it with extra loyalty and effort.

This doesn't mean, of course, that companies aren't worried about the bottom line anymore. It does mean that the needs and aspirations of employees must become a consideration in all business decisions. As Merck's Perry Christensen explained during one of our interviews, the destination today—where companies want to go—is the same as it has always been. What has changed is the way companies get there.

"What's happened at Merck and at a lot of companies today," Christensen says, "is that we do our best to take a much more balanced approach to work than we've taken in the past. Merck is concerned about the numbers; but managers are being judged today not simply on whether they get their numbers or achieve their goals, but on *how* they're doing it: whether or not they are utilizing their people in the best way and whether they're developing their people."

Christensen's comments are worth dwelling upon because they epitomize the theme of the rest of this book: the notion that employees are not interchangeable pieces of equipment, but are critical, long-term assets that need to be treated accordingly.

The argument isn't only philosophical or social; it's economic. If it is true that the key to competitive success in most businesses is doing a better job than your competitors of creating value for your customers, it is equally true that without a stable, highly motivated workforce, that goal will never be met. Which is another way of saying that today, more than ever, there is not only a social or personal payoff to giving more attention to the people side of your business policies; there's an economic payoff as well—and in more ways than one. Even putting aside for the moment the impact that employee turnover has on your ability to meet the needs of your customers, turnover is an expense unto itself. As Christensen pointed out during our interview, Merck's internal studies have shown that whenever an employee leaves the company, for whatever reason, the replacement cost ends up being approximately 1.5 times the annual salary for managers and other nonhourly employees, and three-fourths the annual income for salaried employees.

Basics of Employee Loyalty

How do you go about creating employee loyalty in today's environment, especially when a company is struggling through a loyalty-deficit cycle? I wish I had a simple answer to this question, some magic wand that I could hand you that you could then wave in a lot of different directions late one Friday afternoon, so that on Monday you find all your employee motivation problems have simply vanished.

Unfortunately, there is no such magic stroke, no one technique or strategy that alone can restore the loyalty of the workforce that is in the throes of a loyalty-deficit cycle. Even describing what it takes to create employee loyalty calls to mind the way the seven blind men described an elephant in the Rudyard Kipling tale. One of the blind men felt the elephant's side and said the beast must be very much like a wall. Another grabbed hold of the trunk and likened the creature to a snake. A third, touching the tusk, declared it to be spear-like; while a fourth felt the elephant's ear and stated that it must be a fan; and so on.

So it is with creating of employee loyalty. When you take the time to analyze companies that are successful during this difficult time in keeping their workforces motivated enough to sustain customer loyalty, it quickly becomes clear that there isn't any one program or one device that keeps employees committed and dedicated and willing to go that extra mile for the customer. It's a combination of things—part philosophical and part operational.

One thing, however, is clear: Creating employee loyalty is a concept that is much easier to talk about in the abstract than to translate into a fully operational business strategy.

Therefore, I'll begin this exploration by describing for you, more seriously this time, what *doesn't* work. I am starting out on this negative note to help you avoid some of the common pitfalls to which companies seeking to develop more company loyalty frequently fall victim.

Get Rid of the Bad Apples Approach

There's a tendency among many companies caught up in the loyalty-deficit cycle to blame specific individuals or groups of individuals in the company, the assumption being that the best way to break the loyalty-deficit cycle is to "clean house," to identify and get rid of all the "bad apples"—the people allegedly causing the problems. Why are you getting more complaints than ever about the people in your customer service department? Why is morale so low? Why is turnover so high? Obviously, it's the fault of the supervisor, Miriam. Or Joe. Or whomever.

It may be true that there are more than a few "bad apples" in your company, both in management and on the front lines. And it may also be true, as you will see later on, that to reverse the cycle you have to make some personnel changes, because as long as you have people in your organization who are comfortable with the status quo or feel threatened by change, your efforts to implement real change will be hampered.

In my experience the underlying cause of the loyalty-deficit cycle can only rarely be traced to a single individual or even a group of individuals, the exception being companies in which the founder is the dominant force and has no interest in promoting loyalty. It's almost always the values and work practices that define that culture.

Consequently, unless the changes you intend to make in personnel are driven by a companion effort to institute fundamental, top-to-bottom changes in your culture and in

74 **THE LOYALTY LINK**

your basic work practices, putting new people into the lineup might give you a short-term upswing but probably will not produce any long-term loyalty benefits. Worse, the time and cost of bringing new employees up to speed can actually drain the resources required to get your company back on the right track and moving in the right direction. The key: Your efforts to rebuild loyalty must start with and focus on the people in the organization—here and now.

The Toe-in-the-Water Approach

The loyalty-deficit cycle cannot be dislodged through piecemeal, stopgap approaches. On the contrary, rebuilding loyalty requires a total effort. True, you can't just throw yourself into this initiative without careful planning, but neither can you be timid or equivocal about your intention. The commitment has to be real, visible, and concrete. You don't create loyalty by setting up a loyalty department, or by writing inspiring slogans. You do it through specific actions, meaningful changes that employees can see and experience.

And there is less margin for error than you might think. One of the root causes of declining loyalty in companies, emphasizes credibility authority Jim Kouzes (CEO of the Tom Peters Group and co-author of the best selling book, *Credibility*), is that employees don't trust management to keep its word or to follow through on its initiatives. The so-called social contract that once bonded employees to their companies is no longer a factor in most companies: It loses its relevance whenever a major company announces yet another wave of layoffs and downsizings. Even IBM, a company known for its "cradle-to-grave" employment security is no longer telling employees that their jobs are guaranteed for life. As one high-level IBM executive told me not long ago, "We no longer say to employees, 'we're going to take care of you for life.' We tell them 'do your job well, and we'll reward you.'"

Whether the distrustful feelings that have come to dominate employee-management relations are justified is not the issue here. The fact that distrust exists vastly complicates the challenge of engineering change. Given this environment, anything less than a full and visible commitment on the part of management will often be viewed as a "fad," a flavor-of-the-week approach to employee motivation. Employees simply won't buy it.

You're Empowered, but . . .

Empowerment, as you will come to appreciate in Chapters 7 and 8, is a powerful word and an even more powerful strategy for motivating loyalty and providing more value for your customers. But unless you're prepared to introduce *true* empowerment—that is, to give employees not only added responsibility but the authority, the resources, and the tools needed to carry out that responsibility—you might as well save yourself the time and effort because you're going to cause more problems than you solve.

More about empowerment in later chapters; for now, let me make two quick observations. Real empowerment isn't something you "do." It is something that occurs as a result of what you do, and it takes a long time to be effective. It's a long, bumpy process, and it can be many years before you begin to realize its benefits. Second, if you are serious about empowering your employees, you need to do more than "pronounce" them empowered. You need to make sure they're prepared for their new power. Too many companies ignore this simple but critical principle, and nearly everybody suffers as a result: the employees, the customers, and your company. True, some employees manage to rise to the occasion regardless whether they have been given the support they need, but the effort to do so often results in stress and burnout.

The Buying Loyalty Pitfall

Loyalty isn't something you can buy—not for the long term, anyway. Sure, money talks, but it is abundantly clear from studies in organizational psychology that money alone is rarely enough to keep employees motivated and committed to your business and your customers. Not paying your employees enough can certainly hinder you, but beyond a certain threshold, money alone simply does not create the deep-rooted commitment you need to create and to begin reaping the rewards of a true loyalty-dividend cycle.

Looking Ahead

The four pitfalls I have just described are by no means the only ones companies fall prey to today in their efforts to promote and build more employee loyalty. But they're the most common, and they all spring from the same flawed assumption: that you can win back the loyalty of employees with a single step or single strategy.

To repeat what I said earlier, you can't build or restore employee loyalty in a piecemeal, stopgap fashion. The only way you can hope to break the loyalty-deficit cycle in your company is to attack the problem on not one but several fronts. You need to recognize that in almost every instance, loyalty-deficit cycles are a systemic problem; thus, you need to treat them holistically. Peter Senge, author of *The Fifth Discipline* (Doubleday, 1990), makes this argument convincingly. Throughout the book Senge rails against what he calls "static" or "either-or" thinking, and emphasizes the need to view all efforts designed to produce fundamental change as "processes" and not "trade-offs." Senge notes that for years, American manufacturers labored under the misconception that the price of higher quality was higher costs, and as a result assumed that they had to make a choice between the two. What they didn't consider, Senge maintains, was all the ways that, over time, "increasing quality and reducing costs could go hand in hand." Further he writes:

> What they didn't consider was how basic improvements in work process could eliminate rework, eliminate quality inspectors, reduce customer complaints, lower warranty costs, increase customer loyalty, and reduce advertising and sales promotion costs. They didn't realize that they could have both goals [higher quality, lower costs], if they were willing to wait for one while they focused on the other.

This observation sets the stage for the remainder of this book, as we begin to take a close look at how you can set into motion the initiatives that create a loyalty-dividend cycle. The obvious question we need to focus on, however, is not what companies are doing *wrong*, but what companies benefiting from the loyalty-dividend cycle are doing right. Broadly speaking, I assert that most companies today that fall into this category, regardless of their differences, share the following similarities:

■ They have a strong commitment to helping employees balance the pressures they experience in the workplace with the pressures they experience in their personal lives.

■ They are genuinely committed to the notion of employee empowerment—giving employees more say-so in the way jobs are handled and customers' needs are met.

■ They believe in and have successfully incorporated into their corporate strategy the notion of teamwork and, in particular, the concept of self-managed teams.

■ They have forged a strong link between the internal policies designed to enhance the performance and the dedication of their employees with the specific actions that need to be implemented to take care of customers.

I'm not suggesting that these four general characteristics represent the definitive list of qualities that set loyalty-driven companies apart from other companies. And as you have undoubtedly figured out for yourself, there is a good deal of overlap among these categories. Genuine employee empowerment, for example, can take place only when management values and trusts its employees, and when there are reward mechanisms that keep people motivated. And so forth.

It's worth emphasizing, too, that no one of these four characteristics is more important than any other. All must be present in any effort aimed at restoring employee loyalty. Failing to incorporate or consider the importance of any one of the four will mean that, somewhere along the line, the loyalty link will be weakened. Thus, even as I plot a course through each of these four elements individually, by necessity, what I am describing is actually an organic, dynamic process.

Bear in mind, too, when looking at your own organization, that you may find other elements that are required, depending upon structure, size, industry, or any other factor that makes your company unique. You may also prefer to call these components by other names than those I've given them here. Regardless, these four qualities represent the minimum necessary to create employee loyalty. And these aren't uncharted waters; each can be found at work in organizations that are prospering in this difficult competitive era. The loyalty link is working for them. It can work for you as well.

Chapter 6

Making People Count

The Basics of a Loyalty-Driven Culture

L ike most people, I had never heard of Aaron Feuerstein until I read the newspaper accounts in December 1995 of the explosion and fire that swept through
the factory complex of his Lawrence, Massachusetts-based
textile company, Malden Mills. The fire seriously injured a
dozen of Feuerstein's employees, wiped out 80 percent of
the company's manufacturing capacity, and sent a collective shudder of fear through not only the more than 2,000
local residents who worked at the factory but also through
local government officials and business leaders who knew
that their local economy would be all but destroyed if the
region's number one employer went out of business.

What they feared, logically, was that Feuerstein would
decide that he had had enough, and take the insurance

money and retire to Florida. After all, he was 70 years old at the time and had been directly involved with his business for nearly 50 years. And even if he decided to rebuild, why would he choose to do so in the Merrimack Valley when there were dozens of regions throughout the country promising lucrative tax incentives, warmer weather, and much cheaper labor and energy costs.

But Feuerstein did neither of these things, and that's what turned a local story about a factory fire taking place a couple of weeks before Christmas into national news that struck a responsive chord among people throughout the country.

On the morning after the fire, with the ground still smoldering, Feuerstein gathered a group of employees and union leaders and gave them something that most of them weren't really expecting: reassurance. He told them not only that he fully intended to rebuild the factory, but he was going to do so right there in the Merrimack Valley, on or near the site of the previous one. What's more, he was going to do it in grand style. The new factory, he said, would replicate the nineteenth-century architecture of the original factory, and it would be, as he put it, the "safest, most flexible, environmentally sound factory ever built."

Feuerstein didn't stop there. He promised that when the factory reopened, everybody would have his or her old job back. And he promised that fire or no fire, everyone in the company would receive their Christmas bonuses, that they would be guaranteed, at the very least, a month's pay, and that their health care expenses would be taken care of, at minimum, for the next three months. Little wonder that some employees began to suspect that maybe Feuerstein's real name was Kris Kringle.

From Local Hero to National Symbol

Whether Feuerstein intended to do so or not, his actions following the fire did more than earn him the gratitude of his employees and the businesspeople in the local community. It turned him almost overnight into something of a folk hero. Politicians from all over the state, including the Governor of Massachusetts, William Weld, and the state's two U.S. senators, Ted Kennedy and John Kerrey, flocked to Lawrence to meet and publicly applaud Feuerstein for his humanistic actions. He was lauded by U.S. Secretary of Labor Robert Reich, and he received a personal invitation to attend Bill Clinton's 1996 State of the Union Address. A few months after the fire, Feuerstein received the knitted apparel industry's first annual Man of the Year award. One journalist covering the story suggested that a new award, called the Compassionate Capitalist Award, be created and bestowed upon Feuerstein.

Not everybody, to be sure, was jumping aboard the Feuerstein bandwagon. One textile industry analyst suggested that Feuerstein's plans for rebuilding and considering the welfare of his employees, while noble and ambitious, were too generous; that Malden Mills was taking on far more debt ($300 million) than a company with yearly revenues of $425 million could handle. But Feuerstein didn't debate the economics of his decision. He talked instead about morality and responsibility. "They've been with me for a long time, and they are my greatest assets," he said of his employees. "And we've been good to each other in ways that are not always expressed, except in times of sorrow." He then cited a 2,500-year-old Jewish proverb: "When all is chaos," he said, "that is the time to be a mensch."

Rediscovering a Caring Culture

Mensch is a Yiddish term that, loosely defined, means a decent and responsible person, someone who does the right thing, even thought it may not be in his or her own best interests. Mensch, in other words, was not heard very often during the go-go 1980s, when takeover specialists and venture capitalists were making millions on deals that were putting hundreds of thousands of people out of work. And it's not a word you would use to describe, say, Gordon ("Greed is good!") Gekko, the wheeler-dealer played by Michael Douglas in the movie, Wall Street.

But mensch is a good word to use as the theme of this chapter, for it does a good job of describing a quality that an increasing number of American corporations are suddenly going out of their way to demonstrate these days when it comes to dealing with their employees.

Don't misunderstand. The bottom line is no less important today in business than it was 20 years ago. And it's worth pointing out that apart from whatever humanistic impulses may differentiate Aaron Feuerstein from other corporate leaders, he is—and has always been—an unusual businessman. Unlike many of his longtime competitors in the textile industry, for example, Feuerstein recognized early that he wouldn't be able to compete as an independent company in his industry if he was producing the same products as the bigger fish in his industry. So he decided, long before his competitors, to do what authors like Michael Treacy and Fred Wiersma in The Discipline of Market Leaders (Addison-Wesley, 1995) would advocate years later: to narrow strategic focus, which in the case of Malden Mills meant forgetting about the low-priced commodity fabrics and instead targeting specialty fabrics. Feuerstein geared his operation, equipment, and people toward producing quality fabrics for high-end furniture and clothing companies. And based on newspaper accounts, he was apparently practicing concepts such as "self-directed teams" and "employee empowerment" long before these practices became fashionable. He once described his management team as a "United Nations of talent," a reference to the fact that he had gone out of his way to recruit skilled people from all over the world and to give them a long leash when it came to determining how the company should organize its manufacturing processes. Indeed, one of the breakthroughs that helped Malden Mills develop one of its flagship products—a lightweight fleece fabric known as Polartec that is found in the outerware produced by Lands' End and others—was achieved by a homegrown Malden Mills employee, who had been encouraged ever since he joined the company to be on the lookout for new ways that the company could do a better job of anticipating the needs of its customers.

This point is important because I'm going to be talking a great deal about issues and concerns that have to do with the personal needs of employees, which, in the minds of some people in business today, shouldn't be a priority when it comes to bottom-line decisions, not when profit margins are under such unrelenting pressures. What I will show, though, is that the bottom-line implications of these concerns are greater than ever.

This isn't only my axe to grind. There is a growing realization today among corporate leaders in virtually every industry that paying more attention to the personal needs of employees is no longer something they do out of the goodness of their hearts. It's something they *must* do if they want to attract and retain good employees, enhance productivity, and produce and sustain in those employees attitudes that foster productivity and a strong devotion to their customers. According to Ben Fischer, director of the Center for Labor Studies at Carnegie Mellon University, corporate planners, in a departure from the thinking that dominated most of the 1980s, have begun to abandon the belief that technology would render their workers less important. "It is now broadly acknowledged," says Fischer, "that a corporate strategy requires positive employee attitudes."

That's the good news. The bad news for companies today is that this change in thinking has come about at a time when American employees in general, particularly the survivors in companies that have been wracked by massive downsizings, are more concerned about job security, more distrustful of the motives of their companies, and, according to most surveys, more demoralized than ever before. It also comes at a time when social and demographic factors have combined to intensify a fundamental conflict that has always existed in business but that has now become perhaps the single important issue in human resources today: balancing the pressures of work and family.

As we all know, workers everywhere are finding it more difficult to separate their responsibilities at work from their responsibilities at home. Part of the problem is that the workplace itself has become a more pressured place, with shrinking profit margins, rapidly changing technologies, tighter deadlines, and fewer people to meet the growing demands of customers.

But there's a demographic element to the problem as well. Today's workplace is no longer dominated by men who could come to work each day comfortable in the knowledge that everything was being taken care of on the home front by a full-time homemaker. The Labor Department estimates that by the year 2000, women will account for 47 percent of the nation's workforce, with 60 percent of women of working age having jobs. According to Department of Labor statistics, 42 percent of all working mothers have children under the age of six, a jump of nearly 80 percent above the 1981 numbers, when only one out of four working mothers had young children. At the same time, 71 percent of working mothers, according to surveys, work to support their families.

Add to this mix the fact that people are living longer, resulting in more Americans taking care of an elderly relative, and you can begin to appreciate why child care and elder care have become two of the most widely sought-after employee benefits, second in importance only to health care benefits. You can also begin to appreciate why the work/life balance has become, for many companies, a bottom-line issue. "We really don't have a choice today," is how the human resources director of a Florida-based Fortune 500 company put it recently. "We can no longer pretend that a single mother whose baby-sitter calls in sick at the last moment or a manager who has a parent with Alzheimer's isn't going to allow that pressure to interfere with the work that gets done in the office. People today live much more complicated lives than they used to live, and it's impossible to separate pressures of life and work. And if we don't factor this reality into our planning, we're not going to attract good people, and we're going to burn out the good people we already have."

MAKING PEOPLE COUNT ■ 87

Generally speaking, then, there is no argument. Most corporate leaders today recognize that their companies need to focus more vigorously and more compassionately on the basic "people needs" of their employees, and not just for humanitarian reasons. Employees with the variety of skills needed today to perform well in many industries are becoming harder and harder to find—and keep. Turnover—always a drain on profits—has become an even bigger problem now that there are fewer mentors around to bring new people up to speed. Employee violence also is a concern, in part because of the tensions that have arisen as a result of large-scale layoffs. Companies are also becoming more sensitive to the costs, both direct and indirect, of widespread social problems such as alcoholism and drug abuse. It's now estimated that alcohol and drugs are responsible for as many as 50 percent of the accidents that occur in the workplace today. And it is impossible to calculate the number of accidents that occur because people were thinking more about problems at home rather than on the machine they were operating.

The big question, though, is how to solve these problems. How, in short, do you create a corporate environment that is sensitive to the needs of individual workers but does not jeopardize a company's capacity to compete effectively? More to the point, how do you create this environment at a time when the personal needs of employees are on the upswing and profit margins are on the downswing?

Few questions are more fundamental today to companies seeking to create the critical link between customer loyalty and employee loyalty, and few questions are more difficult to answer. The dilemma is that this problem doesn't lend itself to a by-the-numbers approach, and these are not questions to which you're going to find answers even after you've organized task forces and hired quality-of-life consultants. Questions involving the work/life balance invariably force you to focus on issues that have always been a source of debate and controversy in business and that have no definitive answers, chief among them the nature of the social contract that exists between companies and their employees.

Significant variables of course are values and economics. Not everybody is driven by the same moral imperative as Aaron Feuerstein; then again, not everybody is in a position to make people-related decisions without having to take into account the financial implications of those decisions and their impact on investors and stakeholders other than your employees. Feuerstein conceded that had he been the chairman and CEO of a publicly held company, it would not have been as easy to justify to shareholders, mutual fund managers, and Wall Street the money he was spending to make sure his employees would be reasonably taken care of.

Therefore, throughout this chapter and the rest of this book, I'm not going to frame the issue of the work/life balance in purely moral terms. I'm not going to preach to you about corporate responsibility, or dictate to you what you should and shouldn't be doing for your employees apart from providing them with livable salary and safe working conditions. Instead, I plan to explore this issue within the context of employee loyalty—that is, what you need to do, on a fundamental level, to shape the attitudes that underlie the problems you may now be facing in trying to get more out of your employees. In the end, you'll have to make the decisions that work for you and that meet your particular priorities, whatever they may be. As you read, keep an open mind and be willing to accept the possibility that some of the attitudes you now have and the perceptions you have long harbored may not be as applicable as they were 20 years ago and, without you realizing it, may be sabotaging the very goals you're trying to attain.

The New Standard of Corporate Performance

BusinessWeek ran a cover story recently titled "Balancing Work and Family" (September 16, 1996) in which it singled out 10 companies that had developed "impressive strategies," and were getting "good results" with policies designed to help employees handle the work/family balancing act—without compromising general corporate goals.

The companies were chosen on the basis of a year-long survey that BusinessWeek, in conjunction with Boston University, conducted among some 8,000 employees from 37 corporations that represented a broad cross section of corporate America. The key questions posed to respondents were:

1. What impact does your work have on your home life?
2. Does your company have high-quality programs for employees who have to care for children or elder family members?
3. Can you still have a good family life and get ahead in your company?

4. Is your supervisor flexible when it comes to your work-family needs?

BusinessWeek editors emphasized that they were not positioning this survey as the definitive analysis of work/life balance in America. They admitted, for example, that not every expert in organizational psychology went along with the company's survey methodology; that many large companies (including their own parent company, McGraw-Hill) refused to allow their employees to take part in the survey; and that certain companies that took part but didn't make the top 10 list—AT&T, for instance—may have been penalized because recent downsizings reduced the number of responses.

It's worth mentioning, too, that most of the companies surveyed had large employee populations, which, on the surface, might make the findings of questionable relevance to smaller companies.

These reservations notwithstanding, the *BusinessWeek* report serves as a basis for the key points in this chapter, regardless how large your company is and what sort of business you are in. What comes across loud and clear in this report—and in the observations I've made in companies I've worked with over the past 20 years—is that the main factors that influence employee attitudes and employee loyalty have little to do with the size of the company, and less to do than you might think with how much money you're willing or able to spend on salaries and benefits.

More than anything else, employees must feel they *matter*, that they are not just replaceable parts in a piece of equipment. This does not mean, as I said earlier, that the welfare and well-being of your employees should be your *overriding* priority, overshadowing all the other considerations in your business. Nor does it mean that you don't have the right to fire people who are creating problems for you or not meeting the fundamental requirements of their jobs.

It *does* mean that you recognize how much the success of your business depends on that 40 percent discretionary effort that I talked about earlier; and it means that to achieve this goal, you may have to make an investment, not just in money but in time, effort, and thought.

To help get you started, the following subsections define what most authorities on the work/life balance now agree are the key components of a culture that not only meets the needs of employees but does so in a way that doesn't jeopardize the financial stability of a business.

Make Work/Life Balance a Core Value

Whenever you look at companies doing an effective job of helping employees resolve work/life balance issues, one element is striking. They do more than talk or philosophize about the problem. They're genuinely committed to the principle of doing whatever is reasonably possible to make life easier and more pleasant for their employees. It is a fundamental value, central to the companies' mission, a consideration in all aspects of the companies' business. Motorola, which was ranked second in *BusinessWeek*'s top 10, not only incorporates work/family balance into its mission statement, it has a team of 50 people whose primary job is to travel throughout the company, training supervisors to be more sensitive to personal issues, and making sure that everybody is marching to the same drum. DuPont, also in the top 10, includes "flexible work practices"—a factor that figures prominently in employee attitudes toward their companies—as part of its basic corporate principles. Hewlett-Packard goes even further. If you're the head of a business unit at Hewlett-Packard, you are expected to identify the critical work/family issues that are affecting your division, and you must come up with an action plan as part of your annual business review.

How you go about integrating this value throughout a company is another issue, and nobody claims to possess the magic formula. Clearly, though, the impetus has to originate from the top, and there must be some mechanism—whether it's training or focus groups or regular sermons from senior management—that spreads the gospel throughout the company. More often than not, whether it's a relatively small company like Malden Mills, the Atlanta-based fast-food company Chick-Fil-A, or a corporate giant like Levi Strauss, Eli Lilly, or Hewlett-Packard, there's a direct correlation between a company's work/family policies and the personal values of its leadership.

But it takes more than lofty ideals at the top to make the spirit take hold. According to *BusinessWeek*, this combination of top-echelon buyin, coupled with an intensive and consistent effort to inculcate the value throughout the company, is exactly what is missing in most companies.

"It's an enormous challenge," says Perry Christensen, who helped to spearhead the work/family balance initiative at Merck. "You have to produce fundamental changes in the way many people think. You have to get managers to let go a little bit, to trust people, to treat them as adults, to recognize the multiple priorities that we're all faced with today."

Think Leverage, Not Trade-Off

One of the primary differences between companies that are getting productive results from their work/life initiatives and the companies that aren't is rooted in the fundamental philosophy that underlies the strategy. A recent study initiated by Merck, in conjunction with the Wharton School at the University of Pennsylvania, concluded that one of the principal differences between companies that are doing a good job of helping employees balance their home life and their business life and those that aren't is that they are not bogged down in a "trade-off" mind-set. Progressive companies do not view quality-of-life policies as simply an accommodation, something that management gives up in order to meet certain employee needs. They view these policies instead as a new and better way to do business.

There is nothing wrong or sinister in "trade-off" thinking, but in a report called "Work/Life as a Management Effectiveness Strategy" presented at a Wharton/Merck Work-Life roundtable, researchers who ran in-depth interviews at three New Jersey companies—Merck, Johnson & Johnson, and Allied Signal—found that the trade-off approach, by definition, creates a win-lose scenario. The employee wins when he or she is given time off to attend, say, a parent-teacher conference; but if, as a result of that meeting, work is delayed, the company loses.

A better approach, according to work/life specialists, is embodied in the title of the report: "Work/Life as a

Management Effectiveness Strategy." The idea is that you don't implement work/life balance policies as a "perk" to your employees; instead, you integrate work and personal priorities into a single strategy by which neither the employee nor the company loses.

That's what First Tennessee Bank, which ranked number one in the *BusinessWeek* survey, has done—and with great success. It has used the work/life balance imperative as the first step in a rethinking process. The rationale, as *Business-Week* describes, is to turn the conventional paradigm of work/life balance on its head. Instead of trying to figure out how to make people's lives fit the work, you look for ways to revamp processes so that nobody loses; or, better still, the work gets done more efficiently.

This last concept—the idea of using work/life balancing strategies as a lever to improve processes and build productivity—represents leading-edge thinking, and is very much in line with progressive thinkers such as Peter Senge (*The Fifth Discipline*). The rub, of course, is that it's the most difficult of the strategies to implement and the one most likely to provoke resistance from people who are wed to the status quo.

Be Responsive to Your Employees' Needs

Make sure that whatever policies and programs you establish for your employees in your efforts to enhance the quality of their lives meet the changing needs of today's workplace. Fifteen years ago, for instance, employees in so-called cradle-to-grave companies didn't have to worry about losing their jobs, and consequently, they weren't as interested in learning new skills that would enhance their overall employability. Today, the cradle-to-grave concept is no longer valid. I heard recently about a small manufacturing company in Houston that enjoys an unusually high degree of loyalty because the company's owner offers tutoring and training designed to help its employees launch their own business careers after they leave the company. This concept, sometimes known as *employability*, is catching on and appears to resonate particularly well with younger workers. As one benefits consultant I know puts it, "The idea that you get 'married' to your employees is still operational today. The difference is that both parties pretty much understand that it's no longer a 'til-death-do-us-part' proposition."

Steelcase takes a similar approach, according to Dan Wiljanen. "What we have tried to do," he explains, "is what a lot of companies are saying today; that 'we can't guarantee you a job, or we can't guarantee you lifetime employment, but we can guarantee you employability, if you are willing to work with us.'" Steelcase backs up this promise, Wiljanen says, with programs that help employees develop their careers or personal plans. Employees get feedback on their skills and abilities from their peers, from Steelcase customers, from managers, and from others; the company also offers a tuition reimbursement program. The ultimate responsibility, though, lies with the individual.

Part of a Bigger Picture. Job security today, according to the most recent surveys, is not nearly as important to many employees (younger employees in particular) as two separate but related issues: dependent care (programs or subsidies that help working parents set up child-care arrangements for their children) and flexible scheduling (giving employees the chance to organize their own schedules so that they can coordinate their work hours with school schedules of their children). Most younger workers, for better or worse, wouldn't believe assurances of job security anyway. More important to them is what their companies are doing right now to make life easier for them.

The reason that dependent care has become such an important issue in companies today is, of course, demographic. Now that the two-income household is the rule rather than the exception in America and the number of men and women in the workforce who have young children is mushrooming, dependent care has become not only a business issue but a political issue as well. The pressures that working parents have to deal with in the workplace today were clearly the driving force behind the recently passed Family and Medical Leave Act, which obliges companies to grant a certain number of days of paid leave for employees to deal with family and medical emergencies; and it's an issue that nearly all companies will have to come to grips with in one way or another in the foreseeable future.

Major corporations are dealing with dependent care issues in a variety of ways, but not always with a clear sense of what they're trying to accomplish. Several human resources executives I know confess that their companies are "scared stiff" about this issue. Their companies talk a good game, they tell me, but most are reluctant to take on either the expense or responsibility of providing what some women's advocacy groups are pushing for: on-site day-care centers. At present, only a tiny fraction of the roughly 6 million companies in the United States have specific arrangements for child care that go beyond providing pretax subsidies for working parents, and only a small fraction of that number have on-site care. Many major companies are setting up contracts with outside care agencies. Meanwhile, only about 24 percent of the 8.2 million children under age five who have working mothers are cared for in group centers or nursery schools. For the rest, it's a catch-as-catch-can affair, with children being cared for in home-based centers or by relatives, baby-sitters, or live-in help. Not the best situation for companies seeking to elicit discretionary effort from their key employees.

All of which helps to explain why flexible scheduling has become such a common work practice. According to Hewitt Associates, more than 70 percent of companies in America now offer some form of flextime, reducing the need for working parents to rely on baby-sitters and after-school day care. Here again, companies are being driven not only by a sense of moral responsibility but by a strong economic impetus as well. It has been estimated that absenteeism among working mothers costs companies an estimated $3 billion yearly.

A *Closer Look at Flextime.*   Flextime is one of those rare business ideas that everybody seems to love and that seems to be producing benefits for both employees and their companies. Employees like it, of course, because it helps them organize their lives more efficiently and reduces the conflicts that invariably arise when personal obligations collide with business obligations. But employers, reportedly, are happy as well. Most survey data shows that flexible scheduling reduces turnover and absenteeism and increases productivity. "It's human nature," explains a friend who recently reorganized her work schedule so that she could have two afternoons a week to spend more time with her 7-year-old son. "Once you start taking advantage of the scheduling, you don't want to lose it, and so you tend to work that much harder."

Probably the most interesting aspect of the trend toward flexible scheduling is the ripple effect it is having in companies that instituted it on an experimental, as-needed basis, but have since incorporated it into their fundamental business strategy. First Tennessee Bank—the company that ranked first in the *BusinessWeek* survey—has given many of its departments the freedom to set whatever schedules they see fit. "What we all like about this program," says one First Tennessee clerical employee, "is that we're treated like adults, and it makes us all feel good about working here. It makes me feel good about working here." First Tennessee senior management likes the results. According to *Business-Week*, one specific scheduling change initiated not by management but by a clerical team reduced the turnaround time on statements by 50 percent.

Flextime, however, is no global panacea. It doesn't work equally well in all industries—retailing, for instance—as it does in those in which the work is less time-sensitive. And unless you administer it intelligently and consistently, and get the enthusiastic buyin of supervisors, flexible scheduling can create problems. Human resources managers who've helped department managers formulate flextime policies stress the importance of consistency and determining specific criteria that spell out who can and can't take advantage of flextime scheduling. Without guidelines, you run the risk of creating serious morale problems.

Overall, though, the evidence to date is overwhelmingly positive. Whatever risks you think you may be taking when you give your employees an opportunity to decide for themselves as individuals or as team members when they should work are far outweighed by the benefits you gain in productivity, morale, and loyalty.

The Basics.   One final piece of advice about creating a more people-sensitive environment in your company. Logic would dictate that the best way to find out what your employees need is to ask them directly, but it has been my experience that employees are often afraid—sometimes out of embarrassment and sometimes because they think it will jeopardize their job security—to tell you what they really want. Fortunately there are ways to overcome this obstacle. One way is to interview employees who are leaving the company on their own volition (the logic being that employees who are "out the door" are much more likely to be forthright than current employees). Another approach is to hire an outside consultant, someone who will hold focus groups and can assure employees that everything they say will be kept confidential. (The problem here, though, is that outside consultants can be expensive, and not all employees will trust them to hold to the confidentiality agreement.)

A simpler and less expensive approach is to create a questionnaire that lists the various options (child care, flex scheduling, etc.) and instructs employees to rate, anonymously, the relative importance of each consideration. Be careful though: Don't raise expectations you can't fulfill.

The best thing you can do is the simplest: Put yourself in your employees' shoes. You may not know the specific responsibilities or pressures they face at home (and, by the way, if you have a large company and you probe too much, you could get in trouble with government agencies who enforce discrimination laws), but you can generally get a pretty good idea of their needs simply by looking at the makeup of your employee population, and you can adjust your thinking accordingly. If you have a high percentage of women in your workforce who range in age from early 20s to mid-30s, you can be reasonably sure—without having to probe—that a high percentage of them are married with children. Thus you can be also sure that whatever you do to help them to ease the conflict they invariably feel every time they kiss their children good-bye each morning will go a long way toward enhancing their performance at work.

Simple as this sounds, many companies fail to do this. Two years ago, a major hotel chain launched what it thought was a wonderful initiative designed to improve the English-language skills of its largely Latino service staff. The well-meaning managers who set up the programs were disappointed when only about 20 percent of the eligible employees took advantage of the classes. It never dawned on anybody that the timing of the classes—5:00 P.M. to 7:00 P.M., two days a week—might not be convenient for a woman who was working for minimum wage and, most likely, had one or two children at home.

You can also become more sensitive to the working conditions of your employees. The next time you walk through the office, pay attention to how easy or difficult it is for your computer operators, for example, to operate their equipment. Take some deep breaths and think about how fresh or stale the air is. Pay attention to the noise level: Is it appropriate to the type of work being done? If it's winter and you live in a cold climate, take a look at how many of your employees are wearing extra sweaters. And check out the lighting; and sit in one of the chairs your employees work in and try to imagine how your back would feel if you had to sit there all day. In sum, don't wait for your employees to complain. Do whatever you can, within reason, to address all the various personal needs that can affect their job performance.

To reinforce the value of the exercise I have just described, let me relate a story told to me by one entrepreneur who attended a work/life issues seminar and decided to follow through on one of the recommended exercises. She spent several hours one day going through a simulated version of what the administrative workers in her company experienced each day, from the moment they parked their cars outside to the moment they went home. One of the things she discovered in the course of this exercise was that the frequently used copy machine couldn't have been situated in a less convenient place. It was tucked away in a small airless room, far from where most of the administrative people worked; and because it was so far away and had a tendency to jam, they couldn't just feed it a large-volume job and walk away. They had to stand there. "The chemical fumes were just awful," the entrepreneur told me, adding that no one had ever complained, even though this was clearly a problem for nearly everybody on the staff. My friend went on to say that the simple act of moving the machine to a brighter, more convenient place had a measurable and immediate effect on morale. "What I realize now," she says, "is that just about anything you do that makes it easier for people to do their jobs helps build morale and loyalty."

Walk the Talk

Values are one thing; action is something else again. No surprise, then, that loyalty-driven companies do more than just talk about the importance of the work/family balance.

They have also instituted a set of formalized policies that reflect the core value. Exact figures are hard to come by, but it can be safely said that loyalty-driven companies tend to allocate a higher proportion of their financial resources to quality-of-life issues than companies that are caught in the funk of the loyalty-deficit cycle. It would be wrong to conclude, as I said earlier, that money alone is the answer.

Surveys by Buck Associates, a benefits consulting firm, show that fewer than 50 percent of American employees in large corporations rank money as the number one consideration in job satisfaction. And one striking point in the *BusinessWeek* article—also evident when I work with clients—is how big a difference little things, things that don't necessarily cost a great deal of money, can make in the attitudes of employees and in the degree to which those attitudes translate into better productivity and superior customer service.

Consider, for example, the Seattle-based specialty retailer, Eddie Bauer. Bauer doesn't pay its employees as much as its competitors, but the company still ranked among the top 10 in the *BusinessWeek* survey, primarily because of humane benefits in its corporate headquarters that scored big points with employees. Eddie Bauer is one of a small but growing number of companies that offers specially built lactation rooms, where breast-feeding mothers can pump their milk in private, pleasant surroundings, rather than in a bathroom stall. The company also keeps its cafeteria open after-hours so that late-working employees can pick up a take-home dinner. And Eddie Bauer has also introduced a benefit unheard of when I was working in the human resources department of a major corporation. It's called a "well day"; employees can take one day off *with* pay without having to offer an excuse.

The number of little things you can do to make life easier for your employees (and by little things, I'm talking about gestures and steps that are not part of your formal benefits program and that don't call for significant outlays of either money or time) is almost infinite. Just be creative. Here are a few examples, gleaned from a variety of sources:

- The Pittsburgh-based discount airline Jet Train has installed a washer and dryer in its basement, and reports that approximately 25 percent of its staff use it on a regular basis.

- Andersen Consulting is one of a small but growing number of companies that now offers its busy consultants a "concierge" service. If an employee has to deal with any sort of emergency (a spouse locked the keys in the car, for example) or needs any sort of errand run (dry cleaning picked up, shopping for a party), the employee pays between $5 and $10 (the company picks up the rest of the tab) to a service company that specializes in performing these kinds of services. The corporate strategy, according to one of the company's managing partners, is to relieve the stress experienced by high-performing consultants who typically work 50 and 60 hour weeks, and don't have the time to attend to these little errands themselves.

- A handful of major companies, including Xerox, participate in a program known as Social Leave. Employees who qualify can take a reasonable leave of absence (with full pay and benefits) to work for a nonprofit organization.

- Burger King makes its tuition reimbursement program available to all employees—part-time or full-time—after they have logged at least three months of steady work.

The number of courses paid for by the company is pro-
portionate to the number of hours the employee works
per week.

■ Bell Labs of Murray Hill, New Jersey, arranges for experts
in a wide range of fields (everything from bridge building to bird watching) to come and speak to employees.

■ Quad/Graphics, a printing company in Pewaukee, Wis-
consin, pays employees $30 to attend smoke-cessation
seminars, and gives a $200 bonus to anyone who quits
for a year.

This list could easily go on for pages (several come from
Bob Nelson's excellent book 1001 *Ways to Reward Employees*,
Workman Publishing, 1993). These were chosen with two
general objectives: one, to help you come up with some
ideas of your own; and, two, to emphasize that creating a
more people-oriented environment isn't solely a matter of
writing big checks.

Share the Wealth

How would you feel if you went into work one morning
and found a memo on your desk that made the following
offer: "if the company (not you or your department, but the
company) meets its performance goals over the next year,
you will receive a one-time bonus equal to approximately a
year's pay."

This is precisely the offer that greeted the 37,500 employees of Levi Strauss in June 1996, except that it wasn't presented to employees in a memo, but at a special morning
rally outside the company's headquarters in San Francisco.
The offer was described by the *Los Angeles Times* as the
largest incentive program ever made (it was valued at about

$750 million), but as Levi Strauss & Company Chairman and CEO Robert Haas explained, it was consistent with the company's fundamental values. "Motivated employees are our source of innovation and competitive advantage," Haas said. "By acknowledging and rewarding their efforts, we not only demonstrate our appreciation but also encourage them to continue striving for new standards of excellence."

It may not be possible for your company to make an incentive offer like the one that Levi Strauss made to its employees, but there is no reason you can't learn from the principle at the core of the offer. Apart from its generosity, it meets the three principal criteria for effective incentive programs. Number one, it is attractive to the recipients (Who wouldn't be attracted to an offer that promises a bonus the equivalent of their yearly salary?). Second, the offer seems attainable. And, finally—and perhaps most important—it is an incentive keyed to the long-term goals of the company. As the Los Angeles Times pointed out, Levi Strauss was making a commitment of $750 million, but you can be sure that the number crunchers had calculated that if the company met its financial goals, the money would be there.

No need to belabor the point. Regardless of what you do to create employee loyalty—no matter how "family-friendly" your environment is and how much you pay your employees in salary and in basic benefits—your efforts are not going to bring you optimum results unless you combine them with some mechanisms that give your employees a true sense of ownership, a feeling that their discretionary effort benefits not only the customers but them, too.

The evidence on this point is overwhelming. All the common measures of employee performance (productivity, absenteeism, turnover, customer satisfaction) can be directly correlated to the degree of "ownership" your employees feel. Your employees may like you personally, and they may believe in the product or service that you provide, but "the rubber hits the road" on this particular journey only when you demonstrate, in meaningful terms, that their successful efforts are going to be rewarded. It is no accident that at Springfield ReManufacturing, a company that has become the model of a loyalty-driven manufacturing company, all the employees are owners. "It's a simple principle," says Jack Stack, president and CEO of Springfield ReManufacturing and author of The Great Game of Business, (Doubleday, 1992). "People want to grasp the brass ring. Make it possible, and you'll suddenly get all the loyalty you could ever hope for. It's logic."

Simple in principle, maybe, but not necessarily in execution, especially in companies that are venturing into new, team-oriented ways of doing business. Dan Wiljanen of Steelcase, for instance, admits that his company has "stubbed its toes" a couple of times trying to adapt its bonus and compensation system to the team philosophy it introduced a few years ago. But Steelcase, like most progressive companies, is nonetheless strongly committed to the basic notion of profit sharing. It has a two-tiered system: one is a profit-sharing bonus, based on profitability and issued quarterly; and the other is issued yearly, but again based on profitability. The company sweetens the profit-sharing pie further by making a profit-based contribution to the retirement fund.

Southwest Airlines' program is similar in two key respects: one, the connection of bonuses to profitability; and, two, the timing of the bonuses. But Southwest Airlines adds an element closely tied to its corporate culture: the idea of equality. Every three months, employees who are on the profit-sharing plan—everyone from the company president down to the mechanics—gets a check for the *same* amount. At the end of the year, everybody's salary is added up, and a bonus poll is divided proportionally, with the money then added to a retirement fund. "The key principle," explains Howard Putnam (former CEO of Southwest Airlines and Braniff International), "is—and always has been—to make everybody feel as if they had a stake in the financial success of the company; that everybody is treated equally and fairly."

Almost everywhere you look today both in and out of the Fortune 500 universe, there are fundamental changes in how salaries are set and how bonuses are determined and paid. The trend is away from stratified systems by which pay increases are tied to longevity. Today, more often, salaries and bonuses are keyed to performance and profit.

Also changing rapidly is the way pensions are being handled. Traditional pension plans are gradually being phased out, replaced by 401K plans, in which employers match (in varying proportions) employee contributions. The main difference: In contrast to pension plans, 401K plans are portable; employees don't have to put in 30 years to get something back.

One last point to bear in mind about the money aspect of a loyalty-driven culture: Whatever you do, you must communicate the perception of fairness. Howard Putnam recalls that on the day he was to leave United Airlines to join Southwest Airlines one of the directors of United Airlines gave him a bit of "friendly advice." "Make sure that when you go to Southwest Airlines, that you bring to your board of directors people who make a lot more than you do. That way, when the time comes to ask for your annual raise, they won't be offended by the increase."

"The guy was serious," Putnam says. "He didn't seem to have any idea of how transparent a ploy like that really is. He didn't seem the least bit concerned about how employees might react. And yet, there are a lot of people out there who still think they can get away with it. You can't, not if you want to send the right message to your employees."

Show Your Appreciation

If you work for Bell Atlantic's cellular telephone division in Philadelphia, and you do an outstanding job, the company will sometimes show its appreciation by naming one of its cell sites after you. Perform well at ARA Services, another Philadelphia-based company, and there's a good possibility that the company will honor you with a special day; at the very least, you'll have a free lunch and spend a lot of time accepting the congratulations from other workers and management. If you're a salesperson at KXKT-FM, in Omaha, Nebraska, and you bring in new business, you get to spin a special wheel that gives you a chance to win as much as $1,000. And if you make the grade in Tandem Computer's TOPS (Tandem's Outstanding Performance Program), you could receive an all-expenses-paid trip to Hawaii or the Mardi Gras in New Orleans.

These are just a handful of the thousands of examples I could cite of the many ways that different companies address one of the most fundamental needs we as human beings have, and one of the most powerful weapons you as an employer have to promote loyalty, and make the loyalty work for your business.

The principle couldn't be simpler: Reward good deeds. Give credit where credit is due. And as old-fashioned and obvious as the principle may sound, it works, and works, and works. As Linda McKinley, president and owner of the Atlanta-based Key Temps puts it, "One of the things we're doing constantly in this company is thinking about how to let our good people know how much we appreciate it when they do a good job. We know that if we don't show this appreciation in genuine ways, we're simply not going to get the long-term commitment to meet the needs of our customers."

Virtually everyone I spoke to in connection with this book echoes Linda McKinley's sentiments, in particular, that recognition and credit need to be *constant* and *visible* elements of your corporate environment. By recognizing and awarding achievement, you not only motivate an individual, you send an important message to everyone in your organization. The recognition, moreover, doesn't necessarily have to take the form of monetary rewards. Indeed, as Bob Nelson points out in 1001 *Ways to Reward Employees*, the most powerful recognition-related motivating technique is personal congratulations from a manager—a technique, incidentally, that more than 40 percent of American managers, according to survey data, almost never use.

The specific things you do to credit and recognize outstanding performance in your company—how formal or informal your program is, how much money and time you spend on it, how frequently you put the program into action—are up to you. There is no one model that works for every company, or, for that matter, for every group of employees within a company. For example, it is becoming common practice in certain companies for the chairman or CEO to take the person who has been chosen, say, as Employee of the Quarter to lunch or dinner, but unless the company leader is comfortable in these situations, these get-togethers can be awkward. The lesson: Don't force.

It's important, too, that the system you set up, whatever form it takes, doesn't show favoritism to employees in one particular department—sales, for instance. Chapter 8 explains that the trend in recognition today is toward *group* incentives, reinforcing the critical notion that everybody is important and has a role in satisfying customers.

From a purely strategic perspective, the most important factor in recognition is best described as *customer focus*, making sure that employees see a direct connection between the reward they get and the customer-related impact of the job they've done. Both Jack Stack of Springfield ReManufacturing, and John Case, author of *Open Book Management* (Harper Business, 1995), emphasize that the more employees see specifically how they're contributing to the organization's financial well-being—whether they're sweeping the floor, typing, or developing marketing strategy—the greater the dividend your programs will bring. Perry Christensen agrees, and points out that at Merck, his former company, the entire recognition program is tied into a strategy that combines the company's overall strategies for growth with the objectives that individuals set for themselves to meet broad corporate objectives. Every person in the company, he explains, sets objectives and is then rated according to how he or she succeeded at the end of the year, with credit for contribution given accordingly. A high percentage of Merck employees, moreover, are rated by customers, and they are awarded bonuses based on whether they've created value for the customer.

Another company that lives by the credo of linking recognition with customer-related contribution is MBNA. MBNA, through extensive analysis has quantified 15 key customer service behaviors that have proven to have an impact on generating loyal customers. The company sets benchmarks for performance based on these criteria, and the behaviors are measured and reported on daily to all employees. Most important, MBNA has calculated the value of exceeding the benchmarks, and sets aside bonus dollars (paid out quarterly) for each day the benchmarks are surpassed. Not surprisingly, employees pay close attention to the daily "score," and work hard to gain their credit for contribution.

The main lesson you can glean from the MBNA practice can be summed up in two words: customer impact. Wherever possible, recognition programs should be keyed to the impact that specific employee behaviors have on the customer experience—positive E-gaps. The principle seems obvious, but it's easy to lose sight of. Hal Rosenbuth, CEO of Rosenbuth International, recalls in a 1992 *Harvard Business Review* article that during his first few years in business, the competition for customer-service rewards in his company was so intense that people were, as he put it, "stabbing one another in the back" and creating an environment that, in the long run, was diminishing the quality of the customer service. His response was to retool the program so that employees became less competitive and more team-oriented.

Final Observations

If I have succeeded in driving home a single point in this chapter, I hope it is this: Creating a loyalty-driven culture, one in which people feel respected and valued, isn't only the right thing to do from a human and moral standpoint, it's the smart thing to do from a business standpoint.

It's common sense: The more you help employees feel that you genuinely value them as individuals and don't regard them as robots doing a job, the easier it is going to be for you—everything else being equal—to capture and sustain their loyalty.

This chapter also makes clear that the key issues go beyond salaries and benefits. As Perry Christensen and his human resources colleagues are learning as they examine how the overall corporate environment affects individual performance, it is the "power of simple things." "In the end," he says, "it comes down to trust and openness; whether employees can talk about the issues that are going on in their personal life without having to worry about job security or performance assessments. It has taken a lot of companies more time than it should to recognize it, but gestures as seemingly simple as a manager showing concern about how an employee's child is doing in school or how one of the employee's parents is doing after an operation tends to shape the employee's attitude not just to the manager but the company as a whole. We found in our focus groups that simple incidents that may have taken place 15 or 20 years ago stick in the minds of employees and serve as defining moments for them in how they relate to the company, in how much loyalty they have, and how much discretionary effort they are willing to give the company."

⊰⊱ ⊰⊱ ⊰⊱ ⊰⊱

Benefits at a Glance

Here is a broad listing of the different types of benefits that companies are now offering their employees to help you develop your own benefits package. Keep in mind that the most important factor in benefits today is flexibility—giving employees a range of benefits that they can tailor to their particular needs. Doing so may involve a little more work and effort on your part, but it doesn't necessarily have to increase the amount of money you're spending.

Adoption benefits
Birthdays (time off)
Business and professional memberships
Cash profit sharing
Civic activities (time off)
Club memberships
Company medical assistance
Company-provided or -subsidized automobiles
Company-provided housing
Company-provided or -subsidized travel
Credit unions
Day-care centers
Death leave
Deferred bonus
Deferred compensation plan
Deferred profit sharing
Dental and eye-care insurance
Discount on company products
Discount on other products
Educational activities (time off)
Education costs
Employment contract
Executive dining room
Financial counseling
Free or subsidized lunches
Group automobile insurance

(continued)

ᘓᘖ ᘓᘖ ᘓᘖ ᘓᘖ

Benefits at a Glance *(Continued)*

Group homeowners insurance
Group legal insurance
Group life insurance
Health maintenance organization fees
Holidays
Home health care
Hospital/surgical/medical insurance
Interest-free loans
Layoff pay
Legal, estate planning, and other professional assistance
Loans of company equipment
Long-term disability benefits
Matching educational, charitable contributions
Nurseries
Nursing home care
Outside medical services
Paid attendance at business, professional, and other
  outside meetings
Parking facilities
Pension
Personal accident insurance
Personal counseling
Personal credit cards
Personal liability insurance
Physical examinations
Physical fitness programs
Political activities (time off)
Preretirement counseling
Price discount plan
Professional activities
Psychiatric services
Recreation facilities, sports activities
Resort facilities
Retirement gratuity
Sabbatical leave
Salary continuation

❄❄❄❄

Benefits at a Glance *(Continued)*

Savings plan
Scholarships for dependents
Severance pay
Sickness and accident insurance
Social Security
Social service sabbaticals
Split-dollar insurance
State disability plans
Stock appreciation rights
Stock bonus plans
Stock option plans (qualified, nonqualified, tandem)
Stock purchase plans
Survivors' benefits
Tax assistance
Training program
Travel accident insurance
Vacations
Weekly indemnity insurance

Chapter 7

⊰⊱ ⊰⊱ ⊰⊱ ⊰⊱

Congratulations, You're Empowered

A Loyalty-Based Look at Employee Empowerment

A n acquaintance who has a high-level marketing job with a pharmaceutical company told me the following story a few years ago, prefacing it (for reasons you'll discover in a moment) with the following comment: "I swear it's true."

My acquaintance—let's call him George—was flown, along with 50 or so of his managerial colleagues, to a resort in Mexico where they underwent a week of intensive training, the purpose of which was to launch what at the time was the hot new management initiative: *employee empowerment*. Faced with flat earnings, a lagging R&D effort, and an increasingly demoralized employee population, George's company did what a lot of major companies were

116

doing in the late 1980s—and, for that matter, are still doing. It hired a consulting firm to find out what was wrong, and subsequently was told what most companies suffering the same problems were told then, and are still being told today: To survive in today's fast-moving global marketplace, you can't run a company as though it were a military unit, regardless of how benevolent you are to your employees. Competition is too stiff, changes are occurring too rapidly, and talented employees, especially younger employees, don't want to work in an atmosphere where their main instruction is to follow orders.

The purpose of the week of training George went through was to introduce managers to the basic principles of empowerment; or, as George expressed it, "They brought us there, essentially, to tell us we shouldn't be kicking people around anymore." The training was fairly typical of that administered to companies seeking to create an empowered workplace. There were workshops, discussions, team-building exercises, and even some one-on-one training, all of it geared to getting the managers in attendance to recognize the value of "letting go," of giving employees more autonomy, and of creating a more "open" style of management. The consultants who planned and ran the program, moreover, went out of their way to emphasize that none of the things they were saying or teaching were meant to be "miracle drugs." Empowerment, the attendees were reminded over and over, was not a panacea; it was a process that took a long time to implement.

Most of the managers who went through the training, George says, needed it badly, for they were the embodiment of the management style the company was seeking to change. Most of them had been personally recruited by the company's chairman and CEO, and in the true spirit of monkey see monkey do, they emulated his authoritarian style. They liked giving orders, and they didn't object to taking orders themselves.

At the same time everybody seemed to recognize that the company's declining fortunes, and the failure of stop-gap measures like downsizing and technology to stem the company's decline, gave them no choice. They knew they had to change, as did the company's chairman and CEO, who did not take part in the training himself but arrived on the final day to deliver the closing message.

As George describes it, the chairman began his speech that morning saying all the right things. He told everyone in the room how pleased he was with the report he had received from the consultants who had conducted the training. He emphasized how much he was committed to the idea of making a "fundamental change in the way we do things." He stressed that the pharmaceutical industry, like all industries, was undergoing enormous change, and that their company desperately needed more innovation, more energy, and newer ways to become responsive to the marketplace. And he promised that "the new empowerment initiative was not one of those 'flavor of the month' management initiatives." "The survival of our company," he said, "depends on our ability to change our ways, to become more open, more participatory, less dogmatic."

And now for the "I swear it's true" part. After the chairman and CEO had finished the "pep talk" segment of his speech, his demeanor changed. He looked around the room with the same steely gaze that senior managers knew all too well, and said: "I expect to see measurable improvement by the next quarter," he said. "And if the numbers

don't get better, a lot of you out there are going to be looking for new jobs."

❧ ❧ ❧ ❧

This story would be funny if it weren't so sad. It speaks
volumes to why the very mention of the word empowerment in some companies today could get you thrown out
the front door, if not from the highest window.

Of course, there is nothing fundamentally flawed about
the basic concept. To the contrary, empowerment is an
extraordinarily strong motivational force in business—in
principle, at least—and an indispensable element of loyalty-
driven culture. The idea behind empowerment is to give
employees a stronger sense of control and "ownership"
over their jobs, the rationale being that the more autonomy
and responsibility people have in their jobs, the more commitment and initiative they're going to bring to those jobs,
and the more productive they're going to be.

Empowerment does not mean that employees are given
carte blanche. Nor does it mean that in an empowerment-
driven culture, there aren't parameters, objectives, job descriptions, and all the other management tools that are
common practice in traditional environments. Neither
does it mean that when you empower employees you are
essentially abdicating your responsibility as a supervisor, a
department head, or an owner; or that, as some people
think, you're letting the people who work for you tell you
how to run *your* department or *your* business.

It *does* mean that, within reason, employees are trusted
and valued enough that their input means something,
which translates to control, to some extent at least, of their
job descriptions; and that they can set their own deadlines

and arrange their own schedules according to how they think the job should be handled, not according to what you think, what a supervisor thinks, or what is written in a set of rules.

As already noted, empowerment initiatives don't lend themselves equally well to every environment and every company. Empowerment initiatives are extremely difficult to launch in companies that are in deep financial trouble or have lost touch with the marketplace. They don't tend to succeed, either, in companies that have a long history of labor-management acrimony; nor do they work well in companies that have operated and flourished in paternalistic environments, where employees have become accustomed to highly structured work practices and have no real desire to assume the responsibilities and the risks that empowerment invariably obliges them to assume. As one productivity consultant puts it, "Empowerment doesn't work unless people want to accept it. Many workers, particularly people who've been on the job for years and years, aren't interested. They don't want to be entrepreneurs. They want to be employees."

In general, though, empowerment works, and it is a critical factor in creating and building the level of employee loyalty that adds value for the customer. Every survey or study I have seen on the subject (and it is an elusive practice to quantify, given its subjectivity) confirms what most of us know from personal experience: that the more personally invested you are in any activity, the more commitment you are going to bring to that activity, and the more productive you're going to be. Employees who work in empowerment-driven environments generally report greater satisfaction in their jobs and a stronger sense of loyalty to their companies than do the employees in traditionally structured companies, everything else being equal. Further, in best-case scenarios, the payoff isn't only in happier employees; it's measurable via increases in productivity, quality, and customer service, much of it the direct result of ideas and suggestions that aren't likely to emerge in traditional environments.

And no wonder. Empowerment speaks directly to that part of us that wants to see some tangible cause and effect between the efforts we put forth and the results we achieve. It feeds the instinct most of us have to take reasonable control over our environment. And it taps into that realm of motivation that represents the difference between going through the motions and going the extra mile.

This being the case, it is reasonable to ask why, when we talk about empowerment to human resources executives in major companies throughout the United States, we don't hear a chorus of success stories. There are plenty of success stories out there, of companies in almost every industry that have made fundamental changes in the way power is wielded and decisions are made, and have benefited mightily as a result of it. More often than not, however, particularly in large, old-line companies, empowerment initiatives have tended to sputter. In some instances, they have exacerbated the problems these initiatives were meant to solve.

The Difference between Empowerment and Added Work

Perry Christensen's insights into empowerment reflect the sentiments of most savvy observers of corporate life today and, thus are worth sharing here. In Christensen's view, empowerment initiatives in many companies haven't really empowered employees in the true sense of the word. They have instead added new responsibilities and duties to their existing workload. Basic corporate structures and attitudes, in other words, haven't really changed in most companies that have launched empowerment initiatives. Rather, the management structure has flattened out, with fewer middle managers to supervise front-line employees, but no fundamental change in the way things are done. "What empowerment has meant to the majority of employees in major corporations today," Christensen says, "isn't more power, it's more work."

Christensen adds that empowerment, like work/life issues, cannot be viewed as a policy or program that is added to an existing structure or set of values. It has to be a value in and of itself. "The real measure of empowerment," he says, "is the impact it has on how work is done, and whether the transfer of control is giving people the power to do their jobs more effectively and to bring to their jobs that discretionary effort that we're all trying to encourage these days. The real goal of empowerment should not be to create more work for people, but to get rid of unnecessary work, the work that doesn't create value for the customer."

Case Studies in Empowerment

Christensen's views go a long way to explaining why empowerment initiatives have fared well in some companies and poorly in others. The conventional wisdom is that when empowerment initiatives stumble, the fault lies with people: union leaders who resist the initiatives, senior managers who fail to give their full support to the initiatives, employees who don't want more empowerment, and turf-minded managers who can't adjust their management styles to the facilitative kind of supervision that empowerment initiatives require.

There is no denying that these conditions frequently prevail in companies that have not been able to realize the dividends that employee empowerment brings. But the bigger issue, in almost every instance, has less to do with personalities and more to do with processes: how they are envisioned. With rare exceptions, companies whose empowerment initiatives have made a significant difference in the areas that count—productivity, customer satisfaction and retention, employee retention, and profit margins—haven't just said to employees, "Congratulations, you're empowered." Instead, these companies have been willing to take a look at their overall work practices ("how work gets done," in Perry Christensen's words) and to make a clear distinction between practices that create value for customers and practices that don't. Once *that* decision has been made, these companies have been willing to use employee input as a key element in the reengineering process, then have made sure that employees whose roles would change under the new system are given the training and the support they need to make it work. As Robert Haas, chairman and CEO of Levi Strauss puts it, "If you're going to make the transition from a traditional command-and-control organization to one more flexible, more entrepreneurial, you need an overall approach that encourages and supports new behaviors."

Levi Strauss

Levi Strauss is a classic example of an empowerment strategy that is working, because it has been carefully planned, then implemented with care and commitment. Haas is the first to admit, for example, that his own company, whose reins he assumed in 1984, had fallen victim to the same malaise that strikes many market leaders: It had become complacent. "Once we established a strong market position years ago," he said in a *Harvard Business Review* interview, "We could get by in a traditional, hierarchical, command-control organization, because change happened so slowly. People's expectations were narrowly defined. They gave their loyalty and their efforts in exchange for being taken care of. They expected information and commands to come down from on high, and they did what they were told."

Levi Strauss, Haas says, in the late 1970s and early 1980s had indeed tried to change its direction. It acquired new companies, diversified, created new brands, and applied the Levi's brand to different kinds of apparel. But none of these initiatives, he says, caught fire with employees: the culture didn't change, and the company was in crisis, its domestic profits eroding, its production capacity out of sync with reality, and its diversification strategy not working well at all.

At first, Haas had no real plan of action. It wasn't until the company, as he puts it, started to "listen hard to our suppliers, our customers, and our own people" that the company changed its focus, going back to its core products and articulating a new set of values that embodied the attitudes the company was trying to instill in its employees. "At Levi," Haas says, "creating an empowered organization meant having everybody—myself included—accept the fact that none of us was the smartest guy on the block, and that we multiplied our own effectiveness by multiplying the effectiveness of other people."

That decision, Haas says, coupled with the company's determination to focus with unwavering consistency on the needs and problems of customers have been the driving factors behind the company's empowerment efforts for the past decade. They have dictated the technology the company has invested in (communication systems, for instance, that help customers manage the replenishment cycle faster and more accurately) and have set the tone for most of the dialogue between managers and employees.

But probably the one factor that has had greater impact than any other on the success of the Levi Strauss empowerment effort has been the structural nature of the initiative, the fact that the company has incorporated into its core values the critical principles of empowerment: honest, open communication between management and employees; the willingness of managers to "let go" and give employees a strong voice in how they organize their work; strong incentives for employees who show initiative; and a strong commitment to providing people with the training they need to be a constructive part of an empowered culture. The bonus and compensation procedure is connected as well. One-third of a manager's raise and other financial rewards at Levi Strauss depends on what Haas describes as "his or her ability to manage 'aspirationally'"—not just on results, but, as Merck now does, on how results were achieved; whether those results were consistent with the needs and aspirations of each manager's set of employees.

From Fast Food to Furniture

Two other employee empowerment case studies reaffirm basic principles that apply across the board to successful empowerment initiatives. One is Taco Bell, the Pepsico subsidiary that specializes in Mexican fast food; the other is D.E. Rowe, a furniture manufacturing company based in Salem, Virginia.

Both companies, for different reasons, were experiencing problems 10 years ago, and both seem to be flourishing today, mainly because of the empowerment strategies they successfully implemented throughout their companies. Naturally, specific strategies differed between the two companies, but there were three fundamental and critical similarities:

1. A process or systems-oriented approach to empowerment—not just more work.
2. Strong support from the highest levels of management.
3. A willingness to give the effort time and support it with appropriate training.

Let's start with Taco Bell. Over the past decade, Taco Bell has chalked up one of the more impressive track records in the fast-food industry, and the company's success has often been credited to the decision it made in the late 1980s to lower its menu prices and to build its marketing around the message of value. That decision no doubt was a key factor in the company's success, but as Leonard Schlesinger and James L. Heskett pointed out several years ago in a *Harvard Business Review* article, Taco Bell's success is not rooted solely in its marketing strategy, but is linked more directly to a number of other key decisions that relate to how the work gets done.

Taco Bell began its initiative in the late 1980s with a clear goal: It wanted its managers to spend the bulk of their time focusing on those aspects of the business that had the most impact on the customer experience. For starters, the regional supervisors stopped making as many on-site visits as had been the practice. They weren't entirely removed from the picture, and the withdrawal was gradual. Generally, though, the supervisory role changed: there was less snooping, direction, and control, balanced with more coaching. The net result: Managers spent less time worrying about what the supervisors thought and more time worrying about satisfying customers.

By reducing the direct involvement of supervisors, Taco Bell did not cut down on the communication between stores and their supervisors. The company simply devised a more efficient way to communicate. It introduced a technologically advanced reporting system, not as a replacement for employee/customer contact but as a tool to streamline the reporting process. The change in procedure saved managers an average of 15 hours a week of paperwork, opening up time for discretionary efforts, thus enabling managers to coach employees more, and focus on aspects of the business that enhanced customer satisfaction. (No one yet has proved that a manager's report-writing skill has any bearing on customer experience.)

There's more. Taco Bell analyzed its manufacturing process and figured out a way to save back-of-the-house personnel approximately 15 hours of "unnecessary" work. The result: More employees could be moved to the front of the house, to better serve customers without increasing overall labor costs.

These fundamental changes soon began producing dividends in all aspects of the business. With more time to focus on the process, managers could do a better job of recruiting, interviewing, and hiring new employees, making sure that they fit the company's hiring criteria, which stressed such values as responsibility and teamwork. More attention to hiring resulted in lower turnover rates, and enabled Taco Bell to offer higher wages than its competitors to its front-line workers, resulting in better service to customers, and so forth—the basics of the loyalty-dividend cycle. As profits and revenues started to grow, managers soon became eligible for bonuses that had the potential of earning them more than 200 percent of their annual salaries.

The Rowe Furniture story is similar in its basic outline and results, but different in its particulars. Rowe is a 42-year-old company whose culture and values, according to a *Washington Post* story in 1994, had traditionally reflected the values and the personality of its astute but autocratic founder, D.E. Rowe, a man who, from all accounts, prided himself on his ability to run a tight ship. Fifty years after its founding, however, the company had a new owner and chairman, who, like most enlightened manufacturing executives today recognized that he couldn't run a good company when his managers and employees were at one another's throats. So he sought the help of a board member who, in turn recommended the services of an organizational consultant, whose first obstacle was the plant manager—a man who had been with the company for nearly 50 years and who immediately told the consultant that his ideas were crazy and there was no way they would work in the company's factories.

Eventually, the consultant was able to win over the plant manager who, though stubborn, was nonetheless willing to give some of the consultant's ideas a chance. The main idea was to bring the company's manufacturing operations into the 1990s, which meant replacing the traditional piecework method in the plant—a system by which workers were paid for each piece of furniture produced, with a premium on speed—with a system that was based more on quality and efficiency. The impact of this change, which didn't come easily, was to create a more collaborative environment in which employees worked together to find new ways to increase productivity; that way, their ability to earn more money in salaries wasn't tied only to increased sales but to cost savings that resulted from greater efficiency in manufacturing processes.

Other innovations included the redesign of the company's order form—an improvement that reportedly saved money and cut down on errors; a floating holiday schedule, which the workers set up themselves; and the new symbol of "open-book" management, detailed postings of the company's financial health.

Has it worked? It would appear so. Since 1991, according to the *Washington Post*, Rowe's furniture shipments have climbed almost 40 percent, and the company has increased its gross profit margin from 19 percent to 25 percent, *without* having to raise its prices. The old antagonism is gone, too ("We really like each other," one vice president told the reporter), and even the old-timers grudgingly admit that the "nutty" ideas are working. As one plant manager put it, "I used to think of my employees as rascals. I figured that most of them didn't have enough sense to come in from the rain. Now I can't believe the incredible things that have been just sitting around in their heads." He added, "We all used to think that you should keep workers like mushrooms, in the dark, and feed them manure and they'd grow, when all along sunshine was the answer."

Lessons Learned

Don't presume based on the case histories I've described here, that there's a "magic potion" quality to empowerment. Hardly. In both of these situations, the empowerment process took a lot of time, planning, and patience. And the process is ongoing. People didn't become empowered overnight; and once the process began to take hold, management didn't take it for granted. Most important, the empowerment process didn't involve only people; it involved processes—the way work was done.

It's important to stress, too, that empowerment, as described in these two examples, was the right answer at the right time for *these* companies, where empowerment programs didn't cause unacceptable safety risks for the employees, the customers, or the community; and in neither case did empowering employees generate unacceptable financial risk, which might be the case in, say, a bank or a brokerage firm. Both companies, in other words, were ready for the change in culture that empowerment brings, and both were fundamentally stable and financially solid enough to weather the temporary upheaval that empowerment (or any fundamental change, for that matter) often brings.

I can't guarantee that if you follow the model exemplified in these examples (or in any of the many other examples that you can read in magazine articles and books about empowerment) your company will successfully circumvent the pitfalls common to the empowerment initiative and begin to enjoy the loyalty dividends, but I can promise that if you give empowerment a chance—that is, make a commitment to the concept, invest in the concept, support it with systems and support functions, go about it in a logical determined way, and give it time—the process will propagate itself.

To get you started, here are some do's and don'ts, based on the practices that prevail in companies I have either worked with or studied. Some of this advice reiterates the themes I've stressed throughout this chapter—particularly the notion of approaching empowerment in a holistic, systems-oriented way—but the principles are so important to employee loyalty that they bear repeating.

Be Ready

Empowerment isn't necessarily the route to take in every business and industry, or in every company within a business. The fundamental conditions must be right; or you have to be willing to change those fundamental conditions. Of particular importance: the nature of your business and the work that is carried out in that business; the relative stability of your company; and, most important perhaps, the culture that currently exists in your company—how receptive to the initiative the employees and supervisors in your company are likely to be and how willing *you* are to give the process a chance to work. "Employee empowerment seemed like a good idea for about 60 days," Postal

Union President Vince Sombrotto told one of the reporters from *Training Magazine* recently. "But then management figured out that it actually meant giving up some of their power and letting workers have their say."

Sombrotto makes an important point. Giving more power to certain people in your organization means that *other* people must give up power. It's a simple matter of physics. At the very least, you as the leader must embark on this initiative with a long-range view and with enough resolve so that you don't retreat when you run into obstacles, which you surely will.

The Power You Give Must Have Teeth

A motivational consultant I know often begins his speeches by explaining to his audience why he and his wife have had such a harmonious relationship over the past 25 years. "She makes all the 'little' decisions," he says, "like where we should live, how we should raise our kids, and where the kids should go to school. I make all the big decisions, like whether the United States should pull its troops out of Bosnia."

I think about that joke often when I'm working with companies that have given their customer-service employees what I call "illusionary power." They tell their customer service reps that they, the reps, are now responsible for solving customer problems; but this form of empowerment rarely includes the freedom to exercise discretionary power, other than to follow a set of guidelines programmed into a computer terminal.

Exactly how much authority you're comfortable giving to the front-line people in your organization is a question that you're going to have to wrestle with yourself; and, as

I suggested earlier, the answer will depend on the business you are in and the financial and other implications of these decisions. If you're the president of a bank that is trying to improve productivity and morale through empowerment programs, no one expects you to give your tellers the authority to okay $100,000 loans to anybody who comes in off the street.

On the other hand, if you take a hard, dollars-and-cents look at certain areas of authority, it might surprise you to discover that the risks to autonomy are not nearly as great as you thought. I know a delicatessen owner who requires his cashiers to ask for the driver's license of any customer who wants to pay for his or her order by check. I have never owned a delicatessen and so I don't know how often one gets burned in this business by bad checks; I do know, however, that many of the people who are obliged to produce their driver's licenses whenever they are short on cash are regular customers and that in most instances, the amount is usually in the neighborhood of $7 or $8— hardly a princely sum. I also know that customers who have to wait in line while the cashier is verifying the identity of customers paying by check aren't happy about the delay.

I would suggest to this delicatessen owner first to take a look at how much he might actually lose as the result of bad checks in any given month if there were no controls; or, at the very least, if the cashiers were empowered to seek identity verification from only those customers they don't know. I would then ask him to estimate the amount of money he might stand to lose if some of his regular customers decided that they didn't want to go through the hassle of producing their driver's license for a check for $6 or $7. My guess is that the numbers would speak for themselves. My point is that if you stop to think about it, there are any number of ways you can empower people at all levels of your organization without seriously jeopardizing your financial health.

Trust People to Do Their Jobs

"Moving to an empowered work culture is not about learning new skills," observes Mark Becker in *Training Magazine* ("Lessons in Empowerment," September 1996). "It's about learning new ways to use more of the skills average workers already have."

Becker's point—which comes across strongly in his article—is that when workers are given a chance to make fundamental decisions about how they should organize their time and do their jobs, they don't need to be trained, per se. "On relatively modest incomes," he points out, "workers evaluate options and finance major purchases like houses, cars, boats, and motorcycles. They plan for retirement, and for college educations for their kids. They negotiate with home-improvement contractors, solve problems with the neighbors, and serve on church or community committees."

Becker is not suggesting (nor am I) that workers who have been newly empowered don't need help and support. His argument is that management doesn't have to hold as tight a leash as many people think. He reinforces this claim through a case study of a municipal utility in Lansing, Michigan, an organization that was able to "transform its organizational landscape" but without elaborate training programs. Instead, he says, empowerment was nurtured at the ground level through a series of small changes that allowed all the stakeholders—the supervisors and the employees—to develop the mutual trust that empowerment requires.

If the situation he analyzes is typical—and I think it is—the Lansing utility's experience demonstrates that when given a chance to assume more control of projects, workers who had previously been at odds with management and supervisors over such policy issues as scheduling and time off suddenly became more project-oriented. As one team member put it, "We were so determined to meet or exceed our schedule that we often found ourselves working through breaks and lunch hours."

Set Boundaries

Regardless of how empowered an environment you seek to create, people still must have boundaries and parameters. The trick is to give your employees a chance to participate in the process that establishes those parameters, based on your business objectives and values you've established.

Here, again, there is no "by the numbers" approach to this process, and, again, the degree to which you allow your employees to establish the ground rules and the boundaries will depend on the kind of business you have, the industry you are in, and how much trust you have in your employees' judgment.

If there is any single key to handling this particular aspect of empowerment—and arguably it is the most difficult element in the process—it is your ability to do more than just articulate your objectives. You must make sure to do so in an open, participatory way that invites your employees to see the wisdom and the rationale behind those objectives.

Challenge the Status Quo

BusinessWeek tells of a Xerox Corporation product-development team in Webster, New York, whose first empowerment decision after it had been given the right to set its own schedules was to ban early-morning and late-night meetings and to eliminate reports, in order to give engineers more time to think. The result, according to BusinessWeek, was "happier engineers, and the first on-time launch of a new product in the company's history."

There is plenty of other anecdotal evidence that conveys a similar message, namely that when it comes to getting work done, there is more than one way to skin the proverbial cat. But the balance can't shift entirely away from the needs of the business. Giving people the right to organize their own schedules should mean more than a trade-off between the supervisor who grudgingly gives up authority and a worker who is happier because he or she has more control over his or her time. The company (and the customers) should benefit, too, but this will happen only in a "leveraged" situation, that is, when the empowerment process produces a new and better approach to getting the work done. We're back again to the point Perry Christensen raised earlier: that the ultimate goal of empowerment is not the reengineering of people's attitudes; it's the reengineering of the work process itself—finding better ways to do things.

Rethink Your Rules

Have you ever wondered why tennis matches are scored in the increments of 15, 30 and 40? Why start with 15 and

why is there a difference of 15 between the first two increments and a difference of only 10 between the second two?
Don't spend too much time pondering the answers to these
questions; there are no definitive answers. Much of tennis
scoring derives from court tennis, but that's not the point.
The point is that tennis is scored that way because, well,
that's the way it has always been.

More often than not, many of the rules that companies
ask their employees to follow are a lot like the scoring rules
of tennis: they are there not because they enable the company to operate efficiently and profitably but because
they're the "rules."

Here's a story that illustrates the point. A woman newly
hired as the CFO of an apparel company noticed that on
the day she was unpacking a portable stereo system to set
up in her office, one of her assistants looked as though
the sky were about to fall. When the CFO began to probe,
she found out that there was a "rule" in the company that
no one was permitted to have a personal radio, although
no one really knew how and why the rule became part of
policy.

Later in the day, the company CEO confirmed that there
was indeed a company rule about personal radios, but that
it was one the CEO had simply "inherited." Eventually, after
talking to some of the old-timers in the company, she got
to the root of the mystery. The rule had been originally
written 20 years ago, when the company was located in
much more cramped headquarters, and workers who didn't
have radios were complaining about the workers who did.
The company had long since moved to more spacious offices, which eliminated the problem, but nobody had both-
ered to change the rule.

Here's another example from a *Detroit News* report about the problems the Mazda factory in Michigan was having retaining the "elite corps" it had brought aboard with great fanfare several years earlier. The group had been hired, or so they had been told, because of their "skills, intelligence, and attitude," but once they began working, many felt demeaned by the rules. One electrician reportedly quit because he resented one rule in particular: that ashtrays in the break rooms had to be returned to the precise spots on the table from which they had been removed. The electrician found such a rule at odds with the personal qualities that had led him to be hired in the first place. Of course, had the ashtray rule been the only issue, he wouldn't have quit, but the general feeling among the group was that their input wasn't valued.

Here's a useful exercise in this regard. On your own or with some of your key people, one-by-one take a look at all the various policies your company asks employees to abide by (assuming you have a formal set of policies). Keep an open mind. Look at each policy and ask yourself: "How does this policy affect our ability to serve the needs of our customers?"

My guess is that you'll be surprised by what you'll find. You'll discover, I promise you, that many of the rules in effect are unnecessary and probably inconsistent with an empowerment initiative. Get rid of them, or at least bring them up to date. Your employees will be happier; and so, in the end, will your customers.

Get Supervisor Buyin

Earlier in this book I mentioned the work that Jim Kouzes has done on the issue of credibility. He has shown convincingly that employees have more trust in their immediate supervisors than they do in their organizations as a whole. That's an important bit of insight, for it means that unless you have the support of those people who are interacting daily with employees, your empowerment initiatives are almost certain to run into resistance. Don't automatically assume that because supervisors seem agreeable to your initiatives that they are, in fact, buying in. Be sensitive to what they're giving up and reassure them that they will have an important role in the new order. People shouldn't view empowerment as a penalty, but as a company initiative from which everyone will benefit. If you don't think you can overcome the resistance yourself—and it is tough to do—hire an outside consultant.

Give It Time

Empowerment initiatives cannot be force-fed to employees who are neither receptive nor equipped to deal with the changes they're being asked to make. So don't rush things. As you'll learn in the next chapter, the Ritz-Carlton hotel chain, which now has empowerment programs in place in virtually all of its properties, spent two years pilot-testing its program in one property, and spent a great deal of time prior to studying the experiences of other companies.

If you're looking for tangible results, you have to think in terms of years. When Motorola launched its empowerment initiatives in the early 1980s—long before most companies had heard of the concept—senior management, according to one Motorola executive, was reconciled to the fact that it would be five years at the very least before the programs began to have a measurable impact on productivity and profits.

Hire Right

Not everybody is cut out to operate effectively in a genuinely empowered environment, and it is probably going to be necessary to take a fresh look at your hiring strategies to make sure that you are giving enough weight to the qualities that hold people in good stead in empowered environments. Functional expertise—how well a person performs a particular task—is not as important in an empowered environment as the ability to solve problems, to communicate, and to work effectively in teams.

Enable, Then Empower

Employees are not truly empowered unless they are first enabled (i.e., have the skills and the support necessary to carry out their responsibilities confidently and efficiently). That's where training and coaching come into play.

If you don't adhere to this simple principle, employees who have been only *empowered* may stumble badly the first time they have an opportunity to exercise that power. Customers will then complain, which will lead supervisors to again tighten the screws. Employees will pull back, and the process will falter, leading doubters to crow, "See, I told you it wouldn't work." It's the classic self-fulfilling prophecy.

I have been involved with corporate training for more than 20 years, initially as part of a major corporation but more recently as head of my own training company; so I'm obviously a big believer in the value of training. I'm forced to admit, though, that what passes for training in many companies today, even those that are determined to empower their employees, falls short on two counts. It doesn't meet the needs of the employees, and it doesn't enhance the company's ability to accomplish business objectives.

But the problem is not with training per se; it is a result of the way the concept is executed. With the exception of strict, function-related training—teaching somebody how to operate a forklift or use a new spreadsheet program—training has historically been viewed by most large companies as a "soft" function, something they did as a company because it sent the right "message" to the employees, and not because it contributed measurably to the bottom line. Thus, whenever companies over the years have been forced to tighten their belts, the squeeze is usually felt in training first. But training isn't necessarily eliminated for purely financial reasons. In one major manufacturing company in Pittsburgh, the president canceled all the training programs scheduled in the third quarter of the year because the company had failed to meet its projections in the previous quarter. The reason for the decision, the president informed employees in a companywide memo, was that the employees hadn't "earned" the right to the training.

Think about that for a moment. Can you imagine hearing a football coach say to his team after they've lost a key game: "Okay, guys, you played lousy today. So we're going to punish you. We're not going to practice all week."

I could easily spend the next 25 pages conveying my own views on how to create and run an effective training program, but the truth is you probably don't need my advice. Just be willing to follow a handful of common-sense principles, such as the following.

Build Training into Your Business Plan.   It is difficult to envision any empowerment initiative in which training and coaching wouldn't play a key part. So rather than waiting to see if newly empowered employees need training, make training an integral part of your overall strategy. When Motorola launched its corporate-wide campaign to create a culture better equipped to deal with the competitive challenges of today's world, it established training as an ongoing priority, and backed it up with the appropriate budget. The result at Motorola is that every business group head is expected to allot a fixed percentage of his or her budget to training and development—even if he or she is cutting costs.

Take the Time to Analyze Your Needs. The time, money, and effort you invest in training will be largely wasted unless it is keyed to three things:

■ The core competencies that underlie the ability to perform a particular job or function effectively;

■ The specific needs of the employees being trained;

■ The connection to business objectives.

Far more training programs than you might imagine violate one or more of these principles, and with predictable results—or I should say nonresults.

There are any number of ways you can gather the information you need to make the right decisions with respect to these criteria. Unfortunately, there are no shortcuts. Surveys and prepackaged assessment tools can help, but nothing takes the place of old-fashioned critical thinking. This means, first of all, taking a careful look at the specific employee behaviors that are necessary to achieve the quality levels you want in each aspect of your business, or to produce the intended customer experience. Once you've developed a clear idea of how, hypothetically, things *ought* to be, you can then begin to work backward and determine which employee skills and attributes will turn your hypothetical scenario into reality.

A good place to start is with your customers. Find out what they're looking for. That was what MBNA did when it set up the customer-related criteria that today form the core of its fundamental business practices. Determine, too—by reading, by going to seminars, or by talking to colleagues—the best practices at other companies that are excelling in your marketplace or in other marketplaces.

In short, be a sponge. And don't be afraid to imitate what others are doing. Do your best as well to instill in everybody connected with your organization this same passion for finding new and better ways of doing things. Part of the job description of a restaurant manager at Cafe Concepts in New York is to make frequent visits to other top restaurants in the city, to always be on the lookout for ideas that might be transferable.

Schedule Training on Company Time. Whenever possible, training should be conducted during work hours, and scheduled in a way that doesn't force employees to "squeeze the training in." The reasons for adhering to this principle are both practical and symbolic. The practical reason is that people who are preoccupied with the day-to-day pressures of their jobs are not likely to absorb the full measure of the training. They may put in the time, but they won't get the benefit, and everybody loses. The symbolic reason is that treating training as though it were an "add-on" sends the wrong message to employees whose ability to assume the responsibilities of empowerment depends on learning new skills.

When we're conducting training sessions in our company, we try to have senior managers in attendance introduce the sessions with more than the standard "hello, how are you, glad you're here" sort of greeting. We ask for a clear explanation why training is important, how it fits into the company's overall strategy, and how determined they are as senior managers to support what is being offered in the training.

Offer Tools, Not Principles.   We know both from our experience as trainers and from documented studies that adults in the workplace do not learn the same way that schoolchildren learn, which means that you can't stand up in a room in front of an overhead and recite a lot of principles. What employees want from their training are practical, easy-to-apply tools and processes that relate specifically to their jobs, their problems, their responsibilities; and they want the opportunity, during the training, to practice and get feedback on the skills they are learning.

Here's a scary statistic: Research reveals that in the typical "event-based" or "sheep-dip" training (bring people in once a year, dip them into the training "pool," and send them on their way) attendees end up using less than 5 percent of what they've been taught. Considering that companies today, according to *Training Magazine*, are spending upward of $40 billion on training, you can understand why so many CEOs take a dim view of the money that is spent each year on training.

This is not to say that the programs are without merit. The problem lies in how the training is organized and presented. With this proviso in mind, it's essential that the consultants you hire to develop and conduct your training be part of the solution and not the problem. Make sure they understand your business. Pay particular attention to the processes consultants use and to their learning philosophy. And don't allow yourself to be too dazzled by four-color training materials—especially when they're from off-the-shelf programs; and remember, too, that if your goal is to gain a competitive advantage over your competition, think twice about bringing in a program that is readily available to anybody who wants to pay the price.

And speaking of price, resist the temptation to send your employees to public seminars whose glossy brochures promise to teach them everything they need to know about team building, time management, or writing in one day—and for only $69. Training is no different from any other product or service you buy: You get what you pay for. Remember, you're making an investment, not incurring an expense.

Follow Up. Formal training programs—one- and two-day seminars—represent only one aspect of the process that equips newly empowered employees with the knowledge and the skills they need to succeed in the roles you're asking them to assume. The other half is ongoing support, involvement, and coaching of managers. With this in mind, follow up every training session you run, even if it's with a series of 30-minute refresher sessions over lunch.

Chapter 8

⅜⅜ ⅜⅜ ⅜⅜ ⅜⅜

Adding Team Power
to the Loyalty Link

W hen *Reader's Digest* decided recently to make a
long-term $20 million deal with the printing
company, R.R. Donnelley & Sons, the reason
was not that Donnelley had underbid everybody else or
had superior technology. What fueled the decision more
than anything else, according to newspaper reports of the
deal, was how impressed the decision makers at *Reader's Digest* were with Donnelley's commitment to a team-oriented
approach to manufacturing.

When Seattle-based Boeing ran into difficulties several
years ago with its 737 and 747 programs, it didn't bring in
a team of outside "experts." It put together a homegrown
"dream team" of employees, who became known as Project
Homework, whose mission was to compare the development processes of the 737 and 747 with those of the company's most profitable airplanes, the 707 and 727. The
result of this team effort, which took three years, was a set

of recommendations, known as "lessons learned" that have since become the basis for team-based work practices on Boeing's newest planes, the 757 and 767.

When United Airlines, in a decision that shocked the advertising community, decided to drop its longtime agency Leo Burnett, it didn't select another agency to take Burnett's place; it chose two, both of which were informed from the start that their ability to maintain the account would depend on how well they partnered with one another.

And when Federal Express gathered a group of its employees to unveil its first multimillion dollar advertising campaign, a maintenance supervisor questioned the logic of the theme, built around the idea that "There's a new airline in the sky—FedEx." Challenged to come up with a better idea, the maintenance supervisor is reported to have said, "The only thing that would matter to me as a customer is that the package absolutely, positively gets there overnight." The result: FedEx dropped its earlier slogan and created its new campaign around the now familiar phrase, "Absolutely, positively overnight."

What's Going On?

A new movement is gathering steam in American business today, one I'm sure you know about. It's about teams, or more precisely, self-directed teams: groups of employees who work together as a self-managed unit, sharing collective responsibility not only for the results of their efforts but for the process and sometimes the payoff as well.

It's not a new idea, per se. Working together as a team has always been a widely promoted value in American companies, which have traditionally viewed their various divisions and departments as teams. It's only recently, however, that the notion of introducing autonomy and collective accountability to groups of employees handling a specific task has begun to take hold as a management practice. The team structures taking shape today in American companies represent a much more broadly evolved version of the quality circle teams that were fashionable during the late 1970s, when American manufacturers tried (without much success) to emulate the Japanese practice of bringing together and forming into teams employees from various disciplines. The groups that were the basis of the quality circle movement were, however, largely ceremonial: They could make suggestions and recommendations, but they had no real power to dictate how the work got done.

The self-directed teams of today—theoretically, at least—are empowered. Yes, they have objectives, they operate within certain parameters, and they have to coordinate their efforts with other groups throughout the company; otherwise, though, they pretty much run their own show.

In a typical self-directed team situation, team members work together to plan how a particular project is going to be handled, what's needed to do the work, and how and when the work is going to be done. In companies that have taken the concept to higher levels, teams also create their own budgets, make their own hiring decisions, determine their own bonus structure, and, increasingly, take certain risks that fall within predetermined boundaries.

A Different Way of Managing

Exactly how widespread the self-directed team trend is today and how committed companies are to this concept is difficult to determine. This is understandable given how difficult it is to differentiate a team that is genuinely self-directed from a group of employees that is known as a team but, in effect, operates according to the more traditional model. There are many success stories—GM's Saturn being the most prominent—but even the most ardent disciples of self-managed teams admit that the concept is still in its infancy, and that even in companies that have embraced the idea, very few teams have achieved what Peter Senge refers to in The Fifth Discipline as "alignment," which he uses to describe when a group of people learn how to function effectively as a whole, as opposed to the typical team effort, in which individuals work hard but usually at cross purposes, with much of the individual effort wasted. "Alignment," Senge writes, "is the necessary condition before empowering the individual will empower the whole team. Empowering the individual when there is a relatively low level of alignment worsens the chaos and makes managing the team even more difficult."

But whether their teams are genuinely aligned or not, the number of major companies that have introduced some form of self-directed team activity is now said to be at around 50 percent. And even acknowledging that the number of companies committed to this concept is a good deal smaller, the movement is clearly gaining momentum and can no longer be dismissed as a "flavor-of-the-month" philosophy. It has taken some organizations longer than others to see the light, naturally, but it is generally acknowledged today that the traditional, top-down, authoritarian style of management (a handful of bosses and a whole lot of employees) is simply out of step in today's world. Younger workers today (talented younger workers, in particular) do not respond well to iron-fisted corporate environments; it's not how they were raised or educated. And even if this weren't the case, the growing complexity and the accelerated pace of change in business today has put a premium on innovation, flexibility, and responsiveness—three qualities that are generally stifled by a corporate environment that obliges employees to simply keep their noses to the grindstone and to follow orders.

Fueling the current trend, too, is that self-directed teams are producing impressive results in companies in a variety of industries. The highly publicized success of Saturn, the GM subsidiary that was structured from the start around a team-based model, has given the concept the kind of real-world, bottom-line credibility that the quality circle movement never achieved. And Saturn is not an isolated case. At Chrysler, 32 percent of the workers, according to one report, operate as part of a team that calls most of its own shots as opposed to taking directions from a supervisor or manager. Other companies moving vigorously toward a team-based work environment include IBM, Motorola, Hewlett-Packard, Steelcase Furniture, Ritz-Carlton, to name just a few, most with impressive results. Study after study has shown that when team-oriented policies have been intelligently implemented, as at Saturn, Chrysler, Motorola, and Hewlett-Packard, all the components of the loyalty-dividend cycle begin to flower. Employment involvement and initiative rise. Productivity and quality go up. Waste is reduced. Customers get better products and service. And the ensuing profits enable companies to reward and motivate employees, stimulating them to develop new ideas.

I can attest to this effect from personal experience. When the office manager left our eight-person company several months ago, I toyed with the idea of hiring a replacement to manage the three people who handle all our administrative functions. I decided instead to give the self-directed team concept a try. I offered the senior person in the administrative group the opportunity to be team leader, emphasizing that she was not going to be the boss in the usual sense of the term; she was going to be the facilitator, helping the group carry out its collective responsibility of setting priorities, establishing work processes, and, in general, managing themselves.

My experiment proved to be instructive—and in ways I didn't expect. It quickly became apparent, for instance, that my former office manager, as good and as dedicated as she was, had handled her job the way many bosses typically handle things. She treated the people who worked for her fairly and always with respect, but she was nonetheless a micromanager. Imbued with a strong sense of responsibility, she was much better at giving directions than she was at sharing knowledge and teaching people how to do things for themselves, which worked well as long as she was around. But when she wasn't, the staff never seemed to be in control. Nobody seemed to care. And one of the minor annoyances in our company had long been that when the office manager wasn't in the office, her staff members were always coming to me or other senior associates with questions about how to do this or where to find that.

The fact that the administrative employees in my company had been deprived of the knowledge they needed to do their jobs effectively came to light as soon as we began our self-directed team initiative. It didn't take the team members long to figure out for themselves two things: what they needed to know; and how to find that information. I

expected the transition to be a bumpy one, and I was prepared to weather the bumps. But I was pleasantly surprised. Within a few days, I began to notice a stronger
sense of esprit de corps in the office. Within a few weeks, I
was being asked fewer questions (staff now had the information themselves), and work that under the old system
would have required somebody else's approval was getting
done without it.

The biggest surprise was how the new system affected
one employee in particular. We had always assumed she
wasn't as committed as the others, but with the advent of
the team approach, she quickly blossomed into a top per-
former. Her attitude changed, and the quality of her work
improved measurably. In short, I became a true believer.

Perhaps you're thinking that's fine for a small company,
where everybody knows one another and the owner can
keep an eye on things. So let's look at how the self-directed
team concept promotes customer loyalty and boosts employee performance in two much larger companies: Saturn
and Ritz-Carlton.

Beaming Down from Saturn.   Probably the most highly publicized of all the companies that have adopted self-managed
teams as a fundamental operating practice is Saturn, the
wholly owned General Motors subsidiary that was formed
in 1983.

The Saturn story is valuable to examine on a number of
counts, starting with the reason the company was formed
in the first place: Both General Motors and the United Automobile Workers Union (UAW) had come to see writing on
the wall. They both had recognized that for GM to regain
the market share it had been losing steadily to Japanese

and European imports, both the union and the company would have to change their stripes. Prior to the introduction of the first Saturn car in 1991, GM's market share had declined from a high of over 60 percent to approximately 33 percent; and the UAW had suffered as well, losing 50 percent of its membership during the same period.

From the start, Saturn was aptly described by its trademark slogan: "A different kind of company; a different kind of car." The main difference in the company part of this slogan was Saturn's structure, which was team-driven from top to bottom—and deliberately so. During the three years of planning that preceded the launching of Saturn, the one point that everybody—GM executives, union leaders, and consultants—made clear was that they wanted to create a structure that would eliminate the animosity that had long characterized GM's relationship with its unions.

When it came time to set up the actual team structure, Saturn, of course, had an enormous advantage over most companies. It didn't have to replace an existing culture; it was able to create its own. Nor did it have to invest a lot of money to retool its basic manufacturing processes to accommodate the new system. Everything about the basic working processes was geared from the start to the team concept. Teams were responsible for planning how the work got done, for setting goals, for hiring, for buying equipment, and for developing budgets.

Significant, too, the planning was focused on little things as well as big things. Symbols became important. There were no "hourly workers" at Saturn; there were "team members," who were paid a salary, not an hourly wage. Compensation was determined, in large part, on performance and profits. Everybody was an "owner." The top priority was customer satisfaction.

Nonbelievers in the automotive industry were quick to point out that for all the hoopla, Saturn hadn't proven that it could hold its own in the fiercely competitive automobile industry, but Saturn's record over the past few years speaks for itself. It has racked up consistently high ratings in J.D. Powers' customer satisfaction surveys, and its profits over the past two years have climbed at a rate that has astonished most analysts. Most significant, though, Saturn has become for many manufacturing companies today the benchmark of the self-managed team concept—proof that it works.

Teamwork, Luxury Style: The Ritz-Carlton Hotel Experience. Ritz-Carlton, the luxury hotel chain, has instituted the self-directed team approaches in most of its 31 properties, and with impressive results, according to a recent report in the trade publication *Hotel and Motel Management.* Since it took its team approach companywide, Ritz-Carlton has reportedly increased job satisfaction, reduced turnover, experienced fewer mishaps, increased productivity, and most important, improved levels of customer service.

And not just microscopically. The turnover rate in one property dropped 36 percent in the first year the program was introduced, then dropped an additional 32 percent in the second year. Employee satisfaction rates during the same time rose from 70 percent to 90 percent.

Ritz-Carlton's experience is also instructive on a number of accounts. Like Saturn, Ritz began with a clearly defined vision of what it wanted to accomplish—a companywide commitment to cooperative efforts that would ultimately translate into better service for the customer. The basic idea, according to its director of corporate training and development, Mary Ann Ollman-Brigis, was to shift the fundamental management approach from one of control and direction to one of facilitation and coaching. The rationale was pure loyalty link, the belief that the real key to meeting its overall business goal, to increase levels of customer satisfaction, was to raise levels of employee commitment and satisfaction.

Once the commitment was made, Ritz-Carlton, like Saturn, didn't just plunge into the drink. Sensitive to its own culture, the consultants and senior managers who were directing the initiative realized that the company had to move with resolve but take into account the sensibilities of its management. So before they introduced the program to the entire corporation, they field-tested it for two years in a couple of properties, making sure that the key people in those properties were foursquare behind the initiative.

Further, as at Saturn, the people responsible for setting up the program at Ritz-Carlton did a good deal of homework, taking the time to investigate what worked and what didn't work at other major corporations such as Federal Express and Xerox that had undertaken team-oriented initiatives. They were careful, at the same time, not to generalize, and to stay focused on the specific needs of their employee population and on their business goals. Most important, they followed through on the initiative. The self-directed team concept isn't a policy that management can implement by decree. It is a living, breathing process that is constantly reinventing itself, changing in response to the marketplace and the growing needs of customers.

Is It Right for You?

My purpose in describing these success stories is not to convince you to introduce the self-directed team concept into your company, but to give you an idea of the mind-set you need to adopt and the steps you need to take if the initiative is going to be successful. It's particularly important that you know what you're getting into, and that you be willing to work your way through the difficulties that will invariably arise. In that regard, the next section explains that motivating people to work together effectively as a self-managed unit does not come naturally to most companies or individuals. You have to work at it, experiment with it, be flexible, and most of all, be willing to make certain fundamental changes in the way you operate and the way you think. The following suggestions will help get you started down a path that is by no means easy to travel but is well worth the journey.

Are You Ready?

Team-concept initiatives are far more difficult to initiate and sustain than empowerment initiatives that focus on individual performance. Thus you must make sure before you start that your ducks are not only in a row but poised to take flight and prepared to evade the volley of shells that will follow.

Most team-building consultants, before they begin the actual business of setting up team structures go to great pains to analyze the culture in place, the objective being to determine just how receptive the climate is likely to be to a team concept. Team structures require fundamental change, which doesn't come easily to most environments, unionized and nonunionized, in which managers and employees have traditionally been at odds. It's not impossible to set up team structures in such environments (Chrysler being the best example), but it makes the transition much more difficult, and requires more forbearance on everyone's part.

Consultants also assess the general financial health of the company, recognizing that team empowerment rarely works as a "last ditch" effort. They look at the current management structure—how stratified it is and how long the people whose power is going to be diminished have been with the company, and how much they stand to lose, financially and psychologically, in the new order. Finally, the consultants—if they are doing their job—put pressure on senior management to determine just how committed they really are to the concept, and how much money, time, and effort they are prepared to invest in the support functions necessary to make the self-directed team concept work.

You don't necessarily need a consultant to tell you whether your company is ready to launch a team-oriented work practice initiative—not if you are willing to take a long, hard objective look at yourself. Chances are, if you have any serious doubts, you're not ready, not now anyway.

Beware of False Assumptions

Many people labor under the assumption that because we are social animals, teamwork comes naturally. It doesn't, certainly not as naturally as in Asian societies, where individuals are conditioned early in life to subjugate their own aspirations to those of the group. The common practice of likening self-directed teams to athletic teams works only to a point. Imagine if you will, a self-managed professional basketball team. Players would decide among themselves who would start, who would play where, and how and when substitutions would take place. I don't see it catching on in the multibillion dollar world of professional sports.

A more accurate metaphor is a repertory theater company, in which the participants decide among themselves which plays to produce; take turns as directors; and learn one another's parts, to make sure that if somebody gets sick, another can step in and play the part.

The point is that you can't just bring a group of people together and assume that the group dynamics are going to develop smoothly. The group process needs to be nurtured. People need practice and help. As Peter Senge reminds us, we still know relatively little about how to create true synergy in a team; that is, how to bring out the best in individuals, and, at the same time, bring out the best in the team.

Be Sensitive to Team Composition

Not everybody, as I have said before, is cut out to be a productive member of a team, and the most effective teams are not necessarily composed of outstanding individuals. On the contrary, outstanding individual performers can sometimes disrupt that sensitive and poorly understood quality known as *team chemistry*.

The most important principle to bear in mind when you're sitting down to figure out the "lineup" of your teams is to focus on the task at hand—not the personalities. There are no absolutes. You may find, once you've analyzed a task, that the people you have on staff may not possess the right mix of skills and knowledge needed to complete it, in which case, you have a difficult choice to make: bring in new people or train those you already have. The better option—as long as it's practical—is to train the people you have (assuming they're receptive). Otherwise, your team-building initiative is likely to be viewed by others in your company as a ruse to get rid of people.

Be sensitive, too, to the fact that some employees will view being invited to be part of a self-directed team as a burden and a sacrifice. We see this phenomenon frequently in the companies we work with that are responding to the growing need to engage in a process known as "team selling." This new selling paradigm—dictated by increasing competition and that more buying decisions are now being made by groups and not individuals—puts less of a premium on a salesperson's one-on-one selling and more of a premium on the ability of that salesperson to orchestrate a team effort, in which people from all over the company (service, finance, etc.) get involved. Many companies seeking to move toward the team model often have to figure out what to do about their "drummers," the top performers who have historically brought home most of the bacon. These superstars, generally speaking, don't like the idea of teaming because they've always done well working as "lone rangers."

The conflict is not easy to resolve, but one company we've worked with did an effective job of integrating its drummers into teams by winning their buyin early in the process. In one situation, the president of the company wrote a personal letter to each of his top sales performers, asking for their help in moving forward on the new initiative. In addition, the president assured the top performers that their salaries and bonuses were not going to be reduced because of the new plan.

Clarify the Team Mission and Expectations

The evidence couldn't be more compelling: Self-directed teams that have a clear understanding of why they've been formed, what their mission is, and within what parameters they have to work are far more likely to succeed than those that are formed with no clear sense of purpose, with no inspiring mission, and with no clear-cut guidelines. You, as the owner, manager, or supervisor need to play a big part in that process. If you're smart, you'll let the team members have a role in formulating the mission statement and setting up parameters.

Whatever you do, don't try to fool anybody. You yourself need to have a clear idea of your long-term business needs and how much autonomy you can truly afford to give any group without putting your company at financial risk or creating problems that will interfere with the ability of other employees in your company to meet their objectives. Companies that have taken a piecemeal approach to the team concept frequently run into internal problems that stem mainly from the friction that arises among members of empowered teams and supervisors who work in areas of the business that do not yet operate on the team concept.

It's largely a communication problem—or more accurately, a lack of communication problem. If you have established self-directed teams in place of the old structure, you must communicate to everyone in the company that individual members of the team, regardless of their position or their title, now have the authority formerly in the hands of a supervisor or manager.

Don't Be Afraid of Diversity

There's an understandable temptation when you're organizing people into self-directed teams to focus on the human side of the process—how well you think everyone will get along. Resist the temptation. Harmony is good, but if the group is too mellow, you end up with the phenomenon generally referred to as a "group think," the tendency of groups to reach decisions that have the full support of members but that do not necessarily represent the best solution to any given problem. The best way to prevent "group think" is to introduce as much diversity as you can into groups, bringing together when appropriate people with different types of expertise and different frames of reference.

Provide the Necessary Support

Imagine what it would be like to be part of a student orchestra where you didn't have enough instruments to go around or had such an imbalance of equipment that the students playing the violin were forced to use drumsticks as bows. Bizarre as it may seem, a great many companies with the best of intentions make this same mistake. With enormous fanfare, they create teams, develop team-oriented mission statements, and preach the gospel of team responsibility. But when it comes to the nitty-gritty, the tools and conditions people need to work effectively as a team, the companies fail to deliver. I've seen team efforts compromised for no other reason than real estate—insufficient office space. I've also seen teams in which four or five people are forced to share the same computer.

I'm not suggesting that the key to success in a team-driven organization is to outfit everybody with the latest state-of-the-art team-building hardware and software. I am suggesting that there's a threshold you need to meet. When members are prevented from doing what they need to do or want to do because they lack the proper tools, you have a prescription for failure.

Keep the Communication Lines Open

Nothing has more bearing on the ability of a self-directed team to perform effectively than the quality and the openness of internal communications. Members of self-directed teams need to interact frequently, both informally and formally, and they need to feel comfortable enough with one another to say what they feel.

Frequency is particularly important. At Ritz-Carlton, for instance, teams do their best to meet on a daily basis, even if it's for 15 minutes. The advantages of frequent meetings are obvious. The more often a group gets together, the more quickly it begins to function as a whole. When teams don't meet often enough, people have a tendency to "do their own thing," and when they finally do get together, a lot of time gets wasted undoing individual endeavors.

If teams can't meet in person, other forms of communication should be implemented. E-mail and programs such as Lotus Notes make intragroup communication easier today than ever, and whenever possible, you should take advantage of them, especially if you're giving team members the option of setting up their own schedules or working from home on occasion.

Seek Commitment, Not Compliance

Some people go into team-oriented management structures with the idea that the way to decide issues is to vote and let the majority rule. That works when you're trying to get consensus about where to hold this year's picnic, but it contributes little to the dynamism you need to generate in a true team-empowered environment.

The problem with the "majority rules" approach to making decisions is that it often penalizes those members of the group who are in the minority and who feel—and often rightly so—that their views are not being taken into account. If the pattern persists, the people who hold minority positions tend to withdraw, thus robbing the group of some of its collective energy.

What's the alternative? Broadly speaking, the process should be designed to produce commitment, not compliance; that is, that makes it the responsibility of the people who hold the majority point of view to win the acceptance and support (if not necessarily a ringing endorsement) of those who aren't already aboard the bandwagon.

This approach requires more time and energy, and at times causes frustration, but, in the end, the decisions that get reached result in actions the entire team can and will support.

Develop a Strategy for Conflict Resolution

The one thing you can bank on when moving toward a more team-oriented environment is conflict. Indeed, if you're not stirring up a lot of conflict and disagreement among your teams, chances are the team is not working at full potential and that its members are falling into their old patterns—letting somebody else make the decisions.

With this inherent problem in mind, you must develop a coherent strategy for resolving conflicts. This, as most team-building consultants will tell you, is probably the most difficult element of integrating a team concept into your company, because most people have never learned the skills necessary to resolve conflict in a way that doesn't damage the fabric of the group. Most people in a conflict situation either try to bully their way to the conclusion, or acquiesce.

Simple rules help. Ritz-Carlton made it a rule early in its self-directed team process that there would be absolutely no finger-pointing and buck-passing in any of the meetings.

Other companies have an unwritten rule that nobody uses the word "I"; it's always "we."

In any event, resolving conflict is difficult, even under the best of circumstances (think about how hard it is in your own family), and you may find it necessary to bring in an outside person to facilitate. Don't view this need as a failure. See it as a step you need to take to make the process work.

Adjust Your Award Structure

Even if you follow to the letter the suggestions I have given you to this point, any attempt to bring team power to your customer loyalty efforts will be scuttled unless you incorporate into your program a salary and bonus mechanism that promotes group effort.

It's widely acknowledged that the majority of companies that have embarked on team-building initiatives have stumbled in this area and are struggling to determine a way to replace the practice of awarding individual effort with one that awards teamwork.

The fundamental quandary is this: How do you create a reward system that motivates members of the team to work as a group without running the risk that certain individuals will feel that their personal efforts are not being recognized? Some companies have attacked this problem by setting up what amounts to a two-tiered system. The emphasis is on group achievement, but with the flexibility that enables group members to reward one another based on individual contributions. It's a sticky wicket no matter how you look at it, but it's not an unsolvable problem, by any means. You simply have to address it; better yet, let your team address it, and come up with the solution. Who knows, the solution could come absolutely, positively overnight.

Chapter 9

❦❦❦❦

Putting the Loyalty Link to Work in Your Company

Whenever I give lectures and workshops that relate to the ideas in this book, I usually talk about my father and how he became successful in the small marina business he bought on the Gulf Coast in Alabama, about the time I went off to college. I don't talk about these things for sentimental reasons; I do it because that small marina business is a good case study in the principles that underlie the loyalty link.

My family's basic business was providing out-of-water storage for boats, but we also provided marine service and fuel to fishermen and private boat owners who didn't store their boats with us; we also had a small shop that sold snacks, drinks, ice, bait, and so forth. What differentiated us from the typical marina is that we didn't have in-water docking spaces. If you were a customer, your boat was put into the water and taken out of the water each time you used it. This arrangement wasn't as convenient as the in-water arrangements other marinas offered, but it was a lot better for the boat and it cut down on day-to-day mainte-nance. And because we were the only out-of-water storage marina in the region, my father, who had operated a num-ber of businesses in Ohio, figured this was a great oppor-tunity, and decided to take advantage of it. It fit the lifestyle he wanted for himself now that he and my mother had become empty-nesters.

The business my father bought was a sick puppy if there ever was one, but he knew that going in. The original owner had founded the business with money he had inherited, but had lost interest over the years and had turned over the reins to a manager whose salary was nearly half the yearly revenues and who had amazingly little interest in the busi-ness, the employees, or the customers.

It showed. Nearly half the marina's storage spaces were empty when my father took over the business. The equip-ment was run down and outdated. The staff was a hodge-podge of part-timers, regulars, and summer hires who came and went, and were content to simply to through the mo-tions and take home their meager paychecks. The business, in short, was dying little by little. If I had known then what I know today, I would have described it as a classic illustra-tion of a loyalty-deficit syndrome.

The Power of Self-Analysis

The first thing my father did was to analyze the business and to figure out what he needed to do to make it suc-cessful. He knew instinctively that there was a market for out-of-water boat storage, which is why he went into the business in the first place. But he also knew that if he was going to meet the needs and expectations of the customers in this marketplace, he would have to make some fundamental changes.

He recognized almost immediately the primary obstacle: that out-of-water storage, valuable a service though it might be to certain boat owners, was more expensive than regular in-water docking and a lot less convenient. This meant that if he wanted the business to succeed, he would have to do two things: keep the customers he already had, and attract new customers, the people who were currently storing their boats in other in-water marinas.

He asked himself a simple question: What, apart from price, were boaters who were storing their boats at in-water marinas getting from the customer experience at the marinas they were now using that they couldn't get from the out-of-water marina he had just bought? He came up with one answer: convenience. If you moored your boat at the typical marina, you could go down to the dock anytime, day or night, and use your boat. At the marina my father bought, the hours were 9:00 A.M. to 5:00 P.M., because the business couldn't afford to pay somebody to be there early in the morning and late at night who could operate the forklift that transferred boats from the water to their storage spaces. And people who kept their boats moored to an in-water dock didn't have to wait the 30 to 45 minutes that it normally took to forklift the boat from the storage space into water, gas it up, and then stock it with bait, drinks, snacks, and all the rest.

My father saw that, if he could make the experience of using our marina more convenient, he could probably attract new customers, not every boater in the region, but certainly those who could afford the extra cost. So he made changes designed to do just that: to make the customer experience more convenient. We began to open at 5:00 A.M. (my shift during the summers when I was home from college) and to close at 9:00 P.M. We also began to offer special services to regulars: they didn't have to go through the normal procedure of waiting 20 minutes for their boats to be put into the water, nor another 10 minutes to get fuel. They could call the marina ahead of time, make a reservation, and have their boat in the water when they arrived. If they wanted, we filled their boat with fuel, stocked their ice chests with cold drinks and ice, and put the necessary bait and tackle in the bait box (depending on which fish were running that week). When they arrived at the marina, they simply went to the dock, signed a slip, and were off for a day of fishing. No waiting. No hassle.

My father did other things as well, all keyed to the same objective: enhancing the quality of the customer experience. He noticed that because of the out-of-the-way location of our shop, customers who came for service at the rear dock had to walk a long distance to buy ice, bait, snacks, or soft drinks. This also meant that the back dock, during peak hours, became so congested with "parkers" that it sometimes took 10 to 15 minutes to get out—not the sort of impression we wanted to give to encourage "drive-by" business. To solve the problem, we built a small outpost-type outlet on the rear dock and stocked it with the most popular items. Almost overnight, the congestion problems disappeared.

My father also noticed that the young men who worked on the dock during the summers—mostly college kids— were about as laid-back as you can get, even by Alabama standards. He pointed out to them that when customers were bringing in their boats at the end of the day, they would probably be in a hurry to get cleaned up, and that if they saw dockhands sauntering, they might interpret the movement as indifference. The dockhands in our marina, he told them, were going to hustle.

My father wasn't happy either with the overall attitude of the employees—and with good reason. Nobody took any pride whatsoever in how the marina looked or operated. To them, it was simply a warehouse for boats. The mechanics who worked in the repair shop felt no sense of urgency (it wasn't *their* boats they were working on). None of the front-line workers made any attempt to really get to know the customers. And nobody paid attention to little things, like keeping the rest rooms cleaned.

Of course, my father could have simply cleaned house— brought in a whole new team. And I'm sure he was tempted to do so, particularly when the employees who were part of the old order kept telling him that all those crazy "Yankee ideas" he was spouting were dogs that wouldn't hunt. Too much bother. Too much work. Not the way things were "done here." Besides, my father was told, it wouldn't make any difference. He would learn soon enough, they said, that local boaters weren't going to pay extra for the out-of-water service, no matter what he did.

My father, let me emphasize, was not a saint and not an especially patient man. But he took a genuine interest in and liked people, and he didn't come from the com-mand-and-control school of management. He was also a good businessman, and he realized that he couldn't grow the business unless he could count on his people. He wanted to own a business, but he didn't want to be a slave to it.

That's why, instead of threatening his employees, he reasoned with them. He got them together and gave them a crash course in Marketing 101, explaining that there was indeed a market out there of additional customers but that the marina was going to have to do things differently to capture that market. He reminded them that the way things had always been done hadn't made the company very successful, nor had it done much for their wages, which were rock-bottom. He explained that more customers would mean more money and profits, which in turn would mean more job security and higher salaries for them. He didn't push or threaten, but he made it clear that this was the direction he wanted to go, and that he was inviting them to be a big part of it. He asked them to give him a chance. He promised that if the business prospered, they would prosper, too.

I would love to report that the buyin came instantly, and that as soon as my father completed his speech, all the employees got together and said, "By golly, he's right. Let's change everything we do." In fact, there was plenty of resistance, lots of false starts, and a good deal of frustration. But my father stayed with it, and gradually things began to turn around.

Employees began to see that the new ideas my father introduced were starting to *work*. The regular boaters were telling their friends about the great service we were offering, and suddenly new customers were showing up. Equally important was that my father "walked the talk." In the beginning, it was my father who was there at 5:00 A.M and who left at 9:00 P.M. It was he who hustled down the docks faster than the younger workers when boaters came in for service. It was he who took a mop and made sure that the rest rooms were sparkling clean. (Eventually, my father never had to tell anybody in the company to keep the place clean. All he had to do was to move in the direction of the mop or broom, and one of the employees would hop to the task—not because they feared my father but because they respected him and didn't expect him to do their job.)

My father was also careful not to overstep. He didn't know much about boat repair, so he went to his mechanic and said, in so many words, "These are my standards. You tell me what you need in the way of support and equipment to meet them, and I'll give it to you."

He demonstrated, too, in tangible ways that he genuinely cared about his employees as people. One of the key employees in the marina was a forklift operator named Smitty, who was married to a woman suffering a chronic illness, and he frequently had to take her back and forth to the hospital. The former manager had always given Smitty a hard time about taking time off to take care of his wife, but my father did the opposite. He made it clear that whenever his wife needed special care, Smitty would be covered and his job would be protected. At the same time, we trained another employee to back up Smitty. Who do you think quickly became the most dedicated and productive employee in the company?

My father was also good about little things that didn't cost a lot of money but that motivated gratitude and loyalty. He was never gushy or intrusive, but he made it his business to take an interest in his employees' personal lives. He knew how many children his employees had, what their names were, where they went to school. He even made it a point to buy them all birthday presents.

He thought of his employees as members of his family, and he treated them accordingly.

Did it work? In the first year, our sales increased 50 percent over the previous year, and we had a waiting list of customers asking for storage space. And things continued on the upswing for the nine years my father ran the company. By the same token, my father was able to achieve his personal objective. Ultimately, he didn't have to be there day in and day out to make sure everybody was doing his or her job. He trusted his employees. He let them do their jobs, and they did them well. We had virtually no turnover. And unlike so many people I know today who run small businesses, my father looked forward to going to work every day. The marina was like a second home—a home that was paying him a nice salary. And when he sold the company, his return on investment was nearly 500 percent.

The reason I have gone into such depth about my father and the family marina business is not to emphasize how brilliant or special my father was, but to drive home the point that there is nothing really new about any of the concepts I've discussed in this book.

Long before people attached names to them, in his own way my father was implementing many of the work practices that you can find today in companies that are reaping the benefits of the loyalty-dividend cycle. He understood intuitively the economics of customer retention, and knew how important it was to understand and exceed customer expectations. He understood what it meant to have a strategic vision and to organize business practices around that vision. He considered the dynamics of work/life balance and saw how much more productive loyal employees could be if he took reasonable steps to resolve their conflicts. He realized how much more people would give when *genuinely* empowered, when given the tools to exercise that power, and when trusted to do their jobs. He knew long before Jim Kouzes drew attention to the principle, that the way to gain the loyalty and trust of employees was to practice what he preached. And, finally, he understood that when it came to producing fundamental change in a work culture, he couldn't force the process, that it would take time; that there were no secret formulas or magic wands, that it had to be worked at.

In this book, I have tried to formalize my father's approach, and by doing so, express what is working in companies throughout the world that have created loyalty-driven cultures. I have tried to show above all that this approach is not only viable to maintaining a competitive edge, but necessary as well.

Restating the Principles

In each of the preceding chapters, I have zeroed in on one component of this process; but as I mentioned earlier, you don't forge the loyalty link by doing any *one* thing. You do it by implementing a variety of work practices that are all designed to help you do a better job of managing customer experiences one at a time, over time.

In this chapter, I would like to reiterate some of the key principles emphasized in earlier chapters, to draw a "road map" to follow to make the loyalty link a reality in your company.

Embrace the Concept

The first step to creating the loyalty link in your company is to embrace the fundamental business principles that underlie the connection between customer loyalty and employee loyalty.

Work the math. As Frederick Reichheld has shown, if you can cut down on customer defections by only 5 percent (and the typical company loses between 20 and 25 percent of its customer base each year), you end up increasing the lifetime value of an average customer by anywhere from 25 percent to 100 percent. Nissan Motor Corporation found that the average luxury car buyer will spend, on average, about $250,000 throughout his or her lifetime. Nissan also found that if a customer is happy with a Nissan product, he or she is likely to generate through referrals five additional customers. That raises the total to $1.5 million, lifetime, and doesn't include the revenue from the secondary referrals that come from those customers. That's the potential cost of a single defection, and that's why customer retention has become a religion in many companies today.

Once you've embraced the concept yourself, make sure you educate your employees. Our informal polls of executives have found that fewer than half of them have any idea of the real costs of attracting or, more crucial, of losing a customer. In some companies, astoundingly, this information was considered "privileged." How silly. How do you expect to generate discretionary effort when none of the employees in your organization appreciates the economic impact of their day-to-day actions?

Promote the Importance of Ultimate Satisfaction

Make sure that everyone in your organization understands how high the satisfaction bar has been raised in today's marketplace. Remember the Xerox study described in detail in Chapter 1: There was not much correlation between loyalty and customer satisfaction in the 3s and 4s on the typical 1-to-5 satisfaction scale, but a seismic jump beyond the 4 plateau when the customer experience *exceeds* their expectations.

Remember, too, that the only way you can convert those satisfied 4s into loyal 5s is to give them a *compelling* reason to stay loyal—something you do by creating a series of exemplary customer experiences over time. And the only way those experiences are going to happen is if your employees are motivated to go the extra mile—to give you the discretionary effort that everyone is capable of but that many never get around to using.

Focus on the Intended Customer Experience

If forced to name the most important idea in this book, it would be the intended customer experience, what it is, exactly, that you want your customers to do, think, and feel as the result of every interaction they have with your product or your company.

Embedded in this notion is the idea that exemplary experiences—the kind that build true customer loyalty—don't just "happen." Something produces them, some deliberate and usually discretionary effort on the part of one or more employees who care enough about their jobs, about your company, and about the welfare of your customers. A key part of this process is understanding customer expectations and being able to analyze every aspect of your business and to isolate the E-gaps, those interactions where there's a disparity between what your customers expect and what actually happens.

You have to be realistic about this, of course. You have to accept, for example, that some of the experiences you would perhaps like to create for your customers are beyond your capacity, financially or another way. My father could have done any number of things in our marina, for example, that would have knocked the socks off our regulars. We could have included a bottle of free champagne in every ice chest, not charged them for the fuel, and made available to them at no charge the latest in fishing gear. The result would have been the most loyal group of customers in the world, but with a balance statement that was hemorrhaging red ink. It's doubtful that we could have stayed in business for more than a few months. But it wasn't necessary for us to provide these perks. Nobody expected them, nor had a right to expect them. We were exceeding expectations in a manner appropriate to our marketplace and to the expectations of our customers.

This is a key and frequently overlooked principle in business, and you need to factor it into your thinking and your business model. You can't be all things to all people. Not long ago, for instance, I flew to London on British Airways. My ticket cost me $337, round trip. Fifteen rows ahead of me, in first class, was a group of passengers who had a set of expectations that clearly exceeded mine. As well they should, for they had paid $3,000 for their seats. The airline met my expectations by taking care of the basics. The plane took off and landed on time. The airline met the expectations of the first-class passengers (I assume) by offering plusses I couldn't get and didn't expect: a seat that turned into a bed, a pair of pajamas, comfy slippers, all the champagne they could drink, and a limo waiting for them at the airport. Was it worth the extra money? Not to me maybe, but possibly to somebody who was pitching a $5 million deal the next day and wanted to be on his or her game on arrival.

The cardinal rule when envisioning the intended customer experience is to aim high but to keep your targets realistic. Find your own niche: what it is about you and your organization that you can make tangible but is also cost-effective and brings high value to the customer.

I urge you not to gloss over this basic and critical step in the loyalty link process; and I urge you, too, to bring as many of your employees into the process as early as you can manage. Get as much firsthand feedback as you can about what is actually happening when customers interact with your competitors. Challenge your employees (yes, challenge them) to uncover every possible area of your business that might be producing those loyalty-killing negative E-gaps. This may sound masochistic, but it's cathartic as well. It forces you to look at yourself as you really are, and it prevents you from succumbing to the one disease that has killed more companies than any other: complacency.

One more thing. Whenever possible—and without getting too 1984-ish about it—step into the shoes of your customer and see what it's like when someone calls your company: How long is it before someone picks up the phone? I know a restaurant owner who makes it a point to stand occasionally in the background and to focus on one thing when customers walk into his restaurant: He looks at the expression on their faces when they walk up to the reservations desk. He doesn't have to overhear what his host or hostess is saying; all he has to do is see how quickly guests smile—a sure sign that they're being made to feel welcome.

Above all, focus on the *totality* of the customer experience. Keep in mind that the difference between satisfied customers and loyal customers is rarely made up of any one thing, but a series of small things, which may seem insignificant to you but that add up in a way that clearly separates you from the rest of the pack.

Analyze Your Environment

You've probably heard the story of the Little Leaguer who, after dropping three fly balls in the same inning, comes back to the dugout and says to his manager, "There's something wrong with right field. I keep dropping balls." In many companies there *is* something wrong with "right field." They're asking employees to create intended customer experiences at the same time they're obliging them to work in an environment that prevents them from creating these experiences.

When I talk about things being wrong in right field, I'm referring to anything that might conceivably interfere with the ability of your employees to use the skills and knowledge they currently possess to best advantage. Whether you can do anything about these problems is another issue, but you need to be aware of the dynamic at work, otherwise you're doomed to make the same mistakes over and over.

Here's a quick illustration. The owner of a small mail-order fulfillment house was justifiably concerned about an increase in shipping errors—packages being sent to the wrong addresses. His initial impulse was to fire the employee who was handling that particular aspect of the business, but he decided instead to go out to right field and see what it was like to play that position.

It was an instructive exercise. The owner saw instantly that the room where the cartons were being packed was too small to enable efficient packing operations. He found, too, that the person in charge of making sure that packages were going to the right destination was also handling a number of other tasks. Consequently, the owner reorganized the system and found, to his surprise, that the errors stopped occurring—and without his having to bring in a new right-fielder.

You could be facing a similar situation in your company; that is, some structural aspect of your environment or your work practices is making it next to impossible for your employees to meet your expectations. It could be the lack of necessary equipment or that the equipment you have keeps breaking down. It could be the scheduling policies you have, or the prevailing culture in your company. Whatever it is, get to the root of it before you start letting people go. I'm convinced, as my father was, that if we had brought in a new team of employees and made no other changes in the basic operation of our marina, we might have seen a little improvement in the beginning, but in a few months, would have been right back where we started.

One last point, and in some ways, the most important aspect of this particular principle: Be open to new ideas. I've talked a great deal about some of the important and progressive trends taking shape in American corporations—work/life balance, empowerment, self-directed teams. To repeat, there is nothing magical about any of these concepts, but each of them, when implemented intelligently and with a clear eye on the outcome, can make an enormous difference in how your employees perform and how you create value for your customers. Consider these trends with an open mind. It is possible today—and more so than ever thanks to technology—to give employees scheduling flexibility that enables them to better balance the pressures of their work and personal lives. Empowerment encourages initiative and involvement, when it's *true* empowerment. And self-directed teams, difficult as they can sometimes be to integrate into a traditional structure, can produce extraordinary results. But the impetus has to come from you.

Develop Your Resources

Most companies I work with do a pretty good job envisioning the intended customer experience and uncovering E-gaps. The process frequently breaks down when companies fail to take a close look at and address the skill levels, and the knowledge base of the employees responsible for making those experiences happen. Here are some key questions to ponder in this regard:

Are your employees aware of the problem creating the E-gap—that is, where their performance is falling short?

Do your employees understand the standards and expectations necessary to deliver the intended customer experience?

Do employees have the right tools to do the job?

Are there conflicts and obstacles keeping them from doing the job that needs to be done?

Are you rewarding them consciously or unconsciously for *not* doing their jobs?

Have employees been given the proper training; and if so, have they been given the opportunity to practice?

These are not the sorts of questions you can answer off the top of your head, but they are questions you should be asking yourself and your employees before you give up on any individual employee.

I admit that I have a strong bias on this issue, although I try to temper it with common sense and a realistic view of business priorities. I do believe that people *can* be developed. I also believe that businesses on the whole have done a miserable job of capitalizing on the innate drive that all of us have to learn and to do better at our undertakings.

I urge you to at least explore the possibility that the proper mix of training and coaching could go a long way to eliminating negative E-gaps, without having to make wholesale staff changes—with one caveat: Do it right. If your idea of training employees is to ship them off to a one- or two-day seminar (or the in-house equivalent), it isn't going to do much to eliminate E-gaps in your company. The sad fact, as I cited earlier, is that employees who go through the typical training seminars, according to most studies, are able to apply no more than 5 percent—and in some cases not even that much—of what they've been taught.

Yes, these seminars can be valuable, but only when you're willing to follow through on that training and provide day-to-day coaching. It's going to take some time and effort and maybe some expense. But look at the potential payoff. When you take the time and effort to develop the skills of your employees, you give them a gift that can't be measured in dollars and cents. And the fruits of that investment are not only better performance and more initiative, but genuine gratitude—the kind of gratitude that produces loyalty.

Set a Target

If you don't already have one, set aside some time to come up with a short statement (three or four sentences, at most) that spells out who you are as a company, how you create value for your customers, and what beliefs underlie the way you create that value. You'll hear this referred to as a mission statement or a vision statement. Whatever you call it, such a statement is a fundamental tool in any environment in which you're asking people to put forth discretionary effort. As Jack Stack of Springfield ReManufacturing reminds us, "People want to go somewhere. They want to belong to something, and so you have to paint the picture to the entire organization as to where you're going, how they can become involved, how they can participate." That's what a good, strong mission statement does.

The following is an example of a mission statement that could well serve as a model for your company. It comes from Po Folks, the Southern food chain: "We always want to be the friendliest place you'll ever find to bring your family for great-tasting, home-style cooking, served with care and pride in a pleasant home setting at reasonable prices."

Why does this mission statement work so well? Because it meets the following criteria:

■ It's crystal clear and compelling.
■ It spells out what the company expects and what it stands for.
■ It's a moral compass that each employee and manager can use as a guide in decisions and behavior.

Again, as with the intended customer experience, it's a good idea to bring employees as early as possible into the process of defining who you are and where you want to go. Let them ponder the same questions you are:

What is the value you provide for your customers?

What do you do as a company that differentiates you from competitors? (Is it the quality of your products, the depth of your service, the efficiency of your operations?) Which customers are you best equipped to serve (bearing in mind that no company can be all things to all people)? And what is particularly compelling or noble about what you do—something that your employees could get excited about?

Keep your mission statement simple. And if it's important, include your values. Steelcase's mission statement consists largely of simple phrases that articulate the company's basic values. "Tell the truth. Keep commitments. Treat one another with dignity and respect. Protect the environment. Build positive relations." "These are simple things," Dan Wiljanen says, "but they are the values that have built the company."

Keep in mind the real function of a mission statement and why it's so important in a loyalty-driven environment. Your goal in such an environment is not just to instruct but to inspire, to give to your employees something to believe—something, apart from money, that warrants their discretionary effort.

Adopt a Crusade-Like Mentality

Once you've formulated your mission—and it may be an ongoing process—the next challenge is to communicate the heart and soul and the nuts and bolts of that mission to the people throughout your company.

In the typical scenario, companies—big companies, mainly—spend far too much time on the front end of the effort and not enough time on the follow-through, particularly at the grass roots level. Advertising agencies are brought in for the purposes of coming up with catchy slogans, and much time is spent looking at the graphics consistency in placards and banners. Frequently a video is involved—the president or CEO articulating the vision for everybody. Increasingly, there are video-teleconferences.

There is nothing wrong with any of these efforts, as long as they are backed up with a systematic and consistent strategy for making sure the initiative makes an impact on the front lines. The best model to follow when it comes to work practices that generate grassroots support for loyalty-driven initiatives comes from Steelcase, although you don't need to follow the model to the letter to get food results.

Shortly after Steelcase began its campaign to shift from its traditional way of manufacturing—piecework—to a more team-oriented approach, management took an unusual step. The entire management team vacated their spacious executive offices, which occupied the fifth floor of Steelcase's five-story corporate headquarters building, and moved into a smaller space on the fourth floor, renaming the complex "the leadership community."

To reinforce the idea of community, the company divided itself into "neighborhoods." The People neighborhood was shared by the VP of human resources, the VP of community relations, the director of the Steelcase Foundation, and most symbolic of all, the company's CEO. Another neighborhood, known as Assets, housed the head of facilities and real estate, the CFO, and the comptroller. The Market neighborhood housed sales and marketing. The Innovation neighborhood had the product development people.

It may sound gimmicky, almost Disneyesque, but "the rationale was simple," explains Dan Wiljanen. "We figured that if we were going to go out on the shop floor and try to preach the principle of teamwork, we had to exemplify it in our own behavior. We knew that if the rest of the company didn't see us doing what we said they should do, it wasn't going to work."

As part of the new team-based, open-communication initiative, Steelcase key executives are urged to be highly visible. They are expected to visit every site location at least four times a year, not just to give presentations, shake hands, and hold meetings. As Dan Wiljanen puts it, "They put on their coveralls and their hard hats and walk around to everybody on the line, and ask, 'how's it going; is there anything I need to know; how can I help you do your job better?'"

Other progressive companies have similar mechanisms to reinforce the values reflected in their mission statements. Southwest Airlines, for example, has a culture committee, 108 employees from all over the company that serve a staggered two-year term and meet at least twice a year to pool the ideas they've gleaned on the basis of the face-to-face meetings they've had throughout the year with senior managers and front-line employees. Members of this committee are responsible during the course of a typical year to visit four different cities. They're given time off and are paid for doing it.

The point is obvious: Regardless of how well-intentioned or beautifully worded your mission statement is, it will go only as far as you're willing to push it and demonstrate it. I learned that from my father many years ago, and to keep that principle fresh in my mind, I remember him hustling down the docks to take care of a waiting customer. With that kind of behavior, he didn't need a mission statement. His behavior *was* the mission statement.

Make Your Customers Part of the Process

One of the great things about that loyalty-dividend cycle is that once it kicks in, it starts to nourish itself. As employees come to understand their roles and are motivated and given the freedom to go about their tasks with more initiative and involvement, they start to tap into the pool of discretionary effort. Usually, quality and productivity go up; customers notice it, and often show their appreciation with more business or referrals, which reinforces the behaviors that have launched the cycle.

Yes, market pressures and competitive activity can still block your progress, but you are usually better prepared than your competitors to overcome those obstacles. You have far more creative power at your disposal to accept and meet the challenges.

But the loyalty-dividend cycle can still use all the help you can give it, especially in the beginning. And the biggest contribution to the process you can make as a manager or owner is to promote as much customer-employee interaction as you can.

Simply put, the principle is to give those assets (your employees) you have worked so hard to develop a chance to give something back to you and your business. Turn those assets loose on your customers so that they too come to see your employees as valuable. Imagine how much more loyal your customers would be if you could get them to recognize that your employees were, in fact, working for them.

More and more companies are adhering to this principle, taking definitive steps to bring their employees into the selling and servicing loop, but most companies could be doing a lot more.

The operating principle couldn't be simpler. The more your employees see the connection between their actions on the job and the customer experience, the better their performance is likely to be. That's human nature. The former astronaut Charles Duke often described in his lectures how much he and other astronauts at NASA were urged to go out of their way to introduce themselves to all the workers, particularly the people doing what is often considered the most menial of tasks: sewing the zippers in the space suits. "I would show the woman sewing the zippers pictures of my wife and kids," Duke explained. "I wanted her to know that she wasn't simply sewing a zipper. She was doing something that could mean the difference between life and death."

Unfortunately, there is one fly in this healing ointment of customer/employee interaction. It relates to one of the more disquieting findings in the 1995 ACSI Customer Satisfaction survey, namely that satisfaction levels tend to go down as customers have to interact deeper and deeper into your organization, away from the people who have direct responsibility for customer service.

One way of responding to this fact is to figure out how to insulate your customers from contact with anybody other than a handful of people in your organization. Who knows, maybe there's a technology available that would enable you to prevent any phone calls from customers getting through to employees who haven't been "cleared."

The better way is to take simple measures to improve the quality of the communication between customers and your employees, regardless of where the contact occurs. That way, you are *leveraging* your employees.

There are any number of approaches you can take to make your employees more aware of what your customers want and need. Invite customers to your site and introduce them to your employees. Let customers describe to your employees what they need and how your company can do a better job for them. Or reverse the process. The next time a salesperson goes to visit a customer, send somebody else along, from accounting or R&D or the shipping department. Can you think of a better way to eliminate E-gaps that might have been triggered by your shipping procedures than to let your shipping person sit down face to face with the person who receives the shipment? I can't.

Make customer education part of your basic work practices. For example, part of every agenda of every meeting you conduct should focus on one or more of your key customers—and not only when there's a problem. Make it the responsibility of one of your employees—perhaps the salesperson or the service rep who visits that company on a regular basis—to deliver a short report. How are things going in that company? Is business up or down? Have there been any important personnel changes? Have they brought in new technology? Are there opportunities you may not be aware of, or potential problems that you can nip in the bud? If there's any sort of need, you want to be there. The bond tightens.

Use technology to your advantage. Ritz-Carlton does this in an ingenious way. Let's say you're a guest at one of its hotels and you call down with a special request—a hypoallergenic pillow, for instance. Three months later, you check into the Ritz-Carlton in Hong Kong and the person at the front desk says, "We have your hypoallergenic pillow." It's not magic. It's technology: a simple database management, coupled with the understanding of how that technology could be put to use to build customer loyalty.

Chapter 10

Final Thoughts

When I give speeches or conduct workshops I've come to expect something I call the "been there, done that" response. It comes from people who agree, in principle, with everything I have to say about the link between customer loyalty and employee loyalty, but who in many instances have been down many of the roads I've described in this book, have not had the best of experiences, and have honest doubts about whether it's possible to run a successful business around the principle of loyalty.

In their defense, many of these people have indeed been there and done that, but the problem almost invariably lies in how the process was handled Far too often, initiatives have been long on rhetoric but short on vision, action, and follow-through. Too many customer-first initiatives have been saddled with a caveat that says, in effect, "Build a long-term relationship with your customers but don't forget the quarterly numbers." Work/life balance initiatives

have all too often been introduced but never vigorously in-
culcated into the culture, with the result that employees
who take advantage of the initiatives frequently find themselves an ostracized minority. Empowerment, as I stressed
in Chapter 7, has too frequently meant more work. And the
team initiatives launched by many companies over the past
few years have been mishandled in just about every way
you could imagine: missions and roles never clarified; systems never changed to accommodate the new approach;
nobody taking the time or effort to teach people how to
function effectively as a group.

So I'm not surprised when I run into skepticism. And I
wouldn't be surprised, either, if after having read this far,
there is still a nagging voice inside of you saying, "Sure, it
sounds good, but . . . ." How do you make it work when you
find yourself in the classic loyalty-deficit cycle: budgets
being assaulted, employees and management at each
other's throats, everyone putting out fires and protecting
their turf, and nobody really paying enough attention to the
lifeblood of your business: your customers.

If it's any consolation, I've been there and done that; I
know what it's like to be part of a corporation in which management, either consciously or unconsciously, communi-
cates to employees that they're expendable. I've worked for
and in companies in which more care was lavished on the
plants in the lobby and the paintings on the office walls than
on the personal needs of the people who worked in the company. I know what it's like to be part of companies whose approach to lagging profits was not to focus on new ways to
create more value for customers but to come up with financial instruments that would mask the fundamental operating weaknesses. And I went through and somehow managed

to survive two major restructurings. In each case, I was astonished at the disparity between the amount of time management spend in due diligence reviewing all the numbers and worrying about the "deal," and the amount of time they spent thinking about the people who were going to be affected once the deal was done.

I also know what it's like to be the owner of a small business, and so I don't need to be reminded of what it's like to have a payday bearing down on you when you're not sure there will be enough money in the bank, or to deal with bankers who couldn't care less about the progressive work/ life balance practices you've introduced into your company. (How do you explain to a loan officer that one of the reasons you went into business in the first place was that you wanted to create a business whose success would not be measured solely by the numbers on a financial statement but by what was happening to the people inside the organization?)

I'm not, nor have I ever been, an enemy of free enterprise; and I love the business of business. But based on my experiences and the work I have done with companies of every size from multibillion-dollar international corporations to companies whose entire workforce you could squeeze into a Honda Civic, I believe in my bones that the key to customer loyalty is employee loyalty, which is to say that the ultimate asset in business is people.

The people who work for you represent the essence of your competitive advantage—the only aspect of your business that nobody else can replicate. Your competitors, remember, can usually buy the same equipment you use to manufacture your product or deliver your service; execute the same marketing strategy; advertise in the same publications. But they can't duplicate Mary or Joe or Phil or whoever it is in your company that makes you different from your competitors. And as most major companies have come to discover over the past few years, you don't necessarily sharpen your competitive edge by replacing Mary, Joe, or Phil with machines. Machines can't learn, can't anticipate customer needs, can't adjust—and can't give discretionary effort. What you see is what you get. Never anything more.

❀ ❀ ❀

My wife is a weekend gardener. She loves all aspects of gardening—digging the soft soil in the spring, planting neat rows of flowers and vegetable seeds, pulling out weeds, putting down mulch, hoeing in the beds, pruning leggy stems. She loves rainy days, sunny days, hot weather, cold weather. She loves it all.

Creating a loyalty-link culture is a lot like gardening. There are many different aspects to it, some more fun than others, but you have to do all of it (and hopefully find fulfillment and satisfaction in the discipline) or you just can't expect good results. In other words, you may be outstanding at identifying exactly the experience you want your customers to have and you can articulate it clearly. Or you may be a wizard at figuring out how to get your organization to function effectively in teams. But if you don't like to (or don't want to) address some of the other elements required for creating the loyalty link, then you're probably not going to harvest the full bounty from your garden.

You will have a better harvest and fewer problems if you start with good seed or plants. But plant selection isn't just a matter of paying higher prices (although that is certainly one aspect). It's more about having a good understanding of the soil and location where the plant will grow. If the location is shady and damp, you can plant tomatoes there but you'll never get a decent crop, because they can't thrive in that environment. And if you fail to properly prepare the soil, then even the most robust plants will suffer.

So too with your business. The better job you do of selecting the right people based on your needs and their skills, the greater the likelihood that they will yield a good crop of productivity, now and in the future. And the better job you do of preparing the organizational "soil"—your culture and value and vision—the greater the likelihood that all the plants will thrive and grow.

Ultimately, that's what it comes down to. This book has been about creating the loyalty link because it's good for business. I'm confident that I've proven the economics of doing so over and over again. But more important, you should create a loyalty link because it's better for everyone involved—you, your employees, and ultimately, your customers. It's not easy, and there's no surefire, simple way to do it. But I believe that it's worth getting some dirt under your fingernails and your knees muddy to give it a try. See you in the garden!

Index